© 2009 Feierabend Unique Books

Judenpfad 61, 50996 Köln

info@feierabend-unique-books.de

www.feierabend-unique-books.de

Idea & Concept: Peter Feierabend, Marc Wnuck

Production: 12ender, Mannheim | www.12ender.de

Layout & Design: Julia Reiter | www.weiss-raum.de

Coverdesign: Sahba Vadegar | www.sahba-yadegar.blogspot.com

Spine: Charlotte | Skak www.skaks.com

Back and Frontcover: Olivier Arcioli | www.olivier-jean-sebastian.com

printed and bound in China

ISBN 978-3-939998-39-6

zeixs

EXCITING WORLD OF PATTERN DESIGN

FEIERABEND
UNIQUE BOOKS

FOREWORD

Pattern Design

Patterns are everywhere – on paper or cloth, as wallpaper or as wrapping material. Patterns can be strictly abstract and geometrical or concrete, multicoloured or monochrome. Sometimes they serve as a background, sometimes as a coating.

They are usually composed of a recurrent motif – often floral or natural, sometimes abstract. They have in common that they're not meant to be seen as a picture with a focus, nor as the main thing that draws the attention. The purpose of a pattern is mostly to create a mood, a backdrop, a setting for the main thing.

Creating an ideal pattern requires a certain restraint and a good knowledge of colours. Historically, William Morris springs to the mind with his famous quasi-mediaeval designs for panels and textiles.

More recently, the Finnish company Marimekko defined a style that is mostly associated with the sixties, though their influence is still visible today. You'll find traces of both in many of the designs collected in this book.

Regardless if they're stark and restrained, or flowery and colourful – "Pattern Design" features an abundance of patterns of all kinds and dimensions. This time, the focus lies on patterns.

Pattern Design

Die ewige Wiederkehr des immer Gleichen. In der Welt der Tapeten, Teppiche und sonstiger zu bedruckenden Materialien könnte man vielleicht treffender hinzufügen: das sich wiederholende Element gibt der Oberfläche seine Gestalt, und die entsteht durch Pattern Design.

Aber weshalb sind Muster so reizvoll?
Natürlich nicht alle, doch die gut „gemachten" lenken den Blick zumindest kurz auf sich und der Betrachtende ist von dieser Wahrnehmung vorübergehend in den Bann gezogen. Warum?
Sucht man vielleicht ein dem Muster „entgegenstrebendes" Element?

Egal, wie diese Antworten ausfallen werden: es ist die Wirkung, auf die es ankommt. Die Wirkung, auf die hin gestaltet wird. Das Anziehende, das immer da seiende Muster der Tapete, welches dann auch wieder angenehm in den Hintergrund tritt. Je nachdem, mit welcher Aufmerksamkeit, mit welcher visuellen Sensorik man sich auf diese Musterungen einlässt.

Es ist in diesem Bereich des Designs das ausschließliche Zusammenspiel von Farbe und Form, das diese Kunst ausmacht. Das Grundelement, auf welches aufgetragen wird, verschwindet hinter diesen Musterungen fast völlig, will sagen: steht nicht im Zentrum der Betrachtung.

Der Sessel kann in seiner plastischen Form beschwingen, bestechen; die gestaltete Oberfläche bleibt Oberfläche - die Nuance liegt in der Wechselwirkung von Farbe zu Form.

Dieses Buch zeigt viele wundervolle Muster; die unterschiedlicher nicht sein könnten. Doch jede Oberfläche hat ihren ganz eigenen Reiz und wenn man sich von der direkten Ebene etwas löst, so können diese Muster auch „erzählen" - man muss sich nur intensiv genug von diesen einnehmen lassen.

objects

dishes, furniture, food,
books, clothing

13

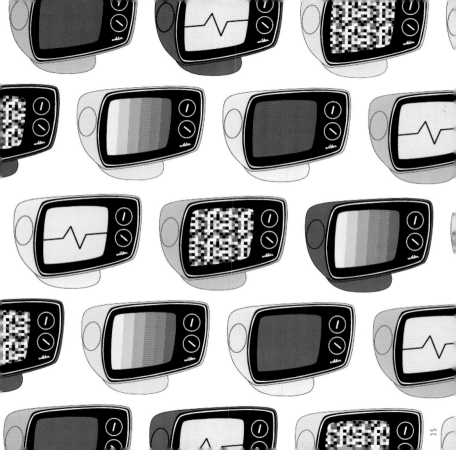

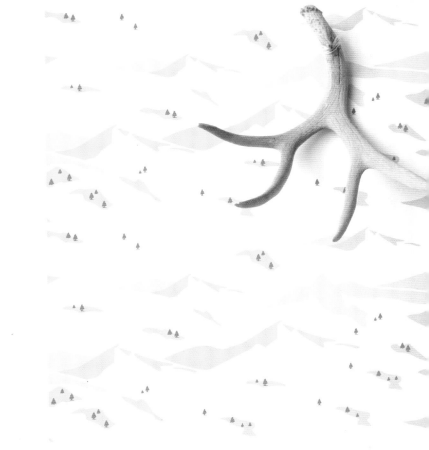

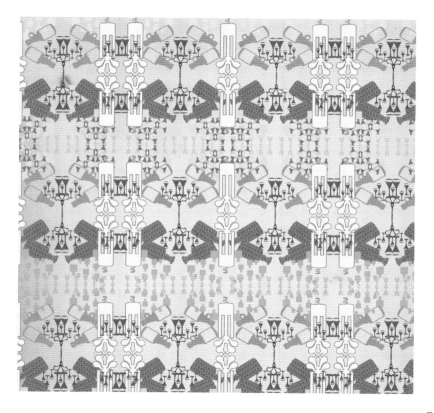

Emil Bertell   (GER)   www.fenotype.com

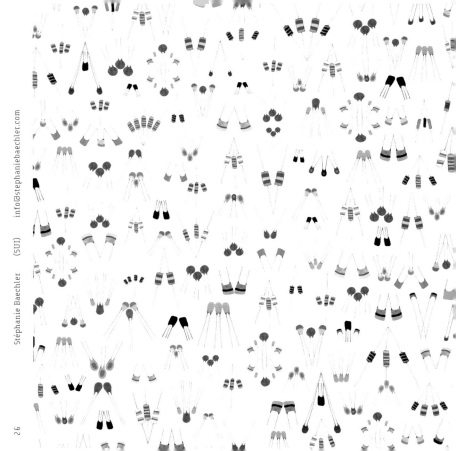

(SUI)

info@stephaniebaechler.com

26

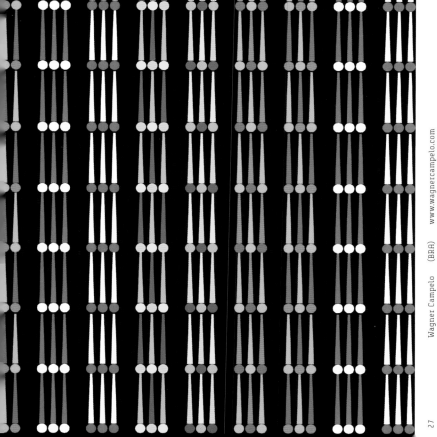

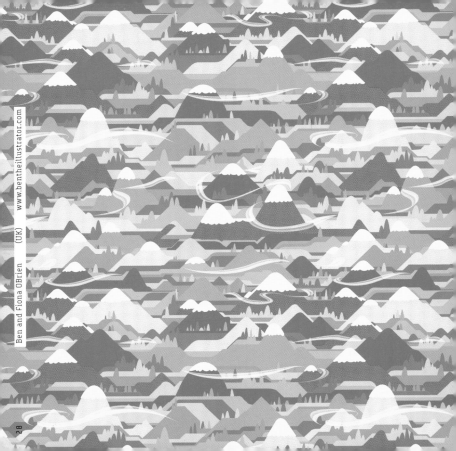

28

THE CONSUMPTION ISSUE

32

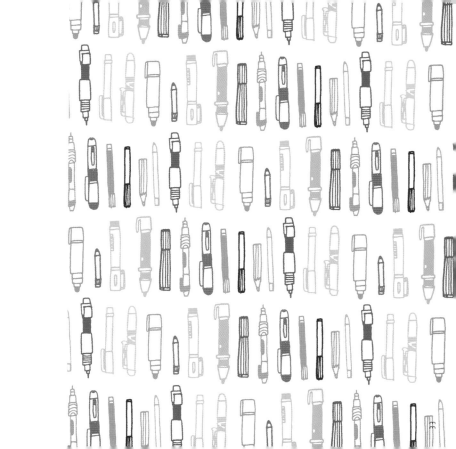

34

38

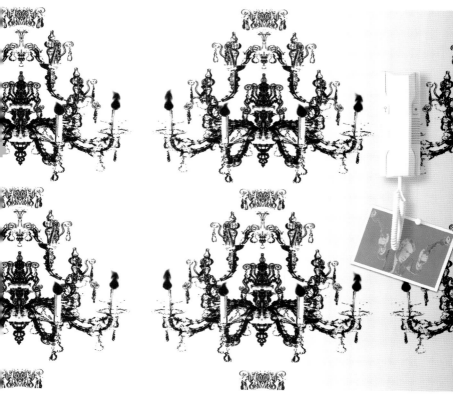

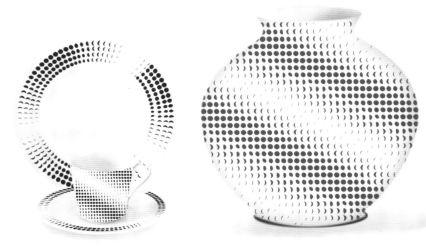

Theresa Scholz (GER)

www.mondphasendesign.de

ちち

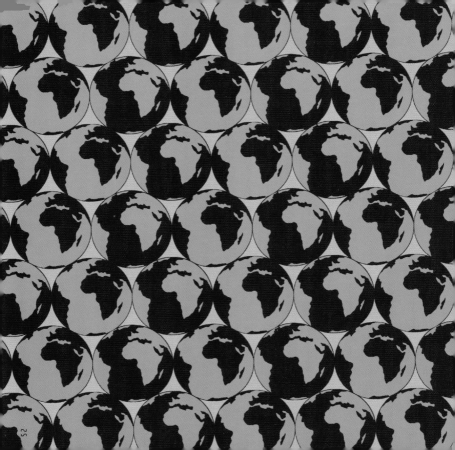

Stefanie Axmann   (GER)   www.stefanieaxmann.com

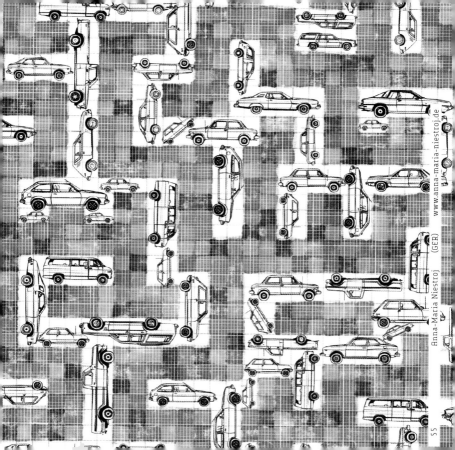

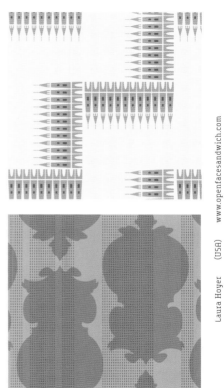

59

Cristina Bocaranda Belisario   (USA)

...ard qui patauge dans la baignoire,
...eubles cubistes, un cactus au large
...es bottes roses qui prennent la fuite
...nts bruts, une biche en pointillés
...s chromatiques mouvants
...vir l'univers de Frenchieslitchies.
...par deux graphistes indépendants
...s, photographiques.
...l'édition, d'illustration,
...de tendances

...renchieslitchies.fr

FRENCHIESLITCHIES
www.frenchieslitchies.fr
design graphique / illustration
hello@frenchieslitchies.fr

Itxaso Torrontegui Palacios (ESP Itxaso_Torrontegui@gmail.com

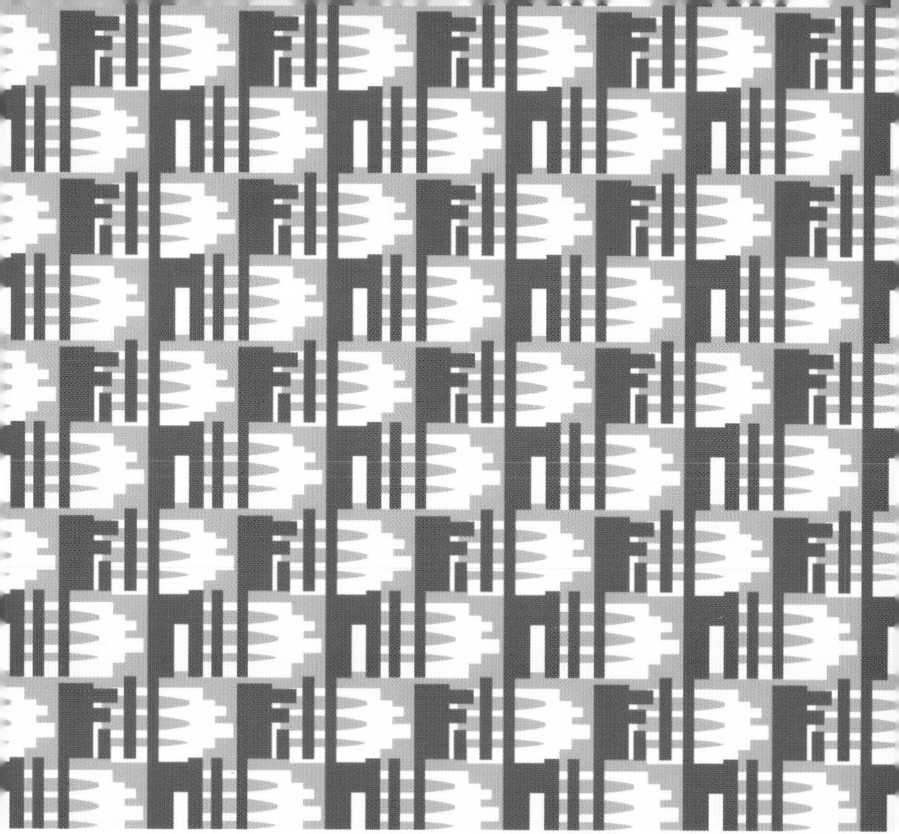

Laura Hoyer (USA) www.openfacesandwich.com

Oliver Melzer   (GER)   www.olivermelzer.de

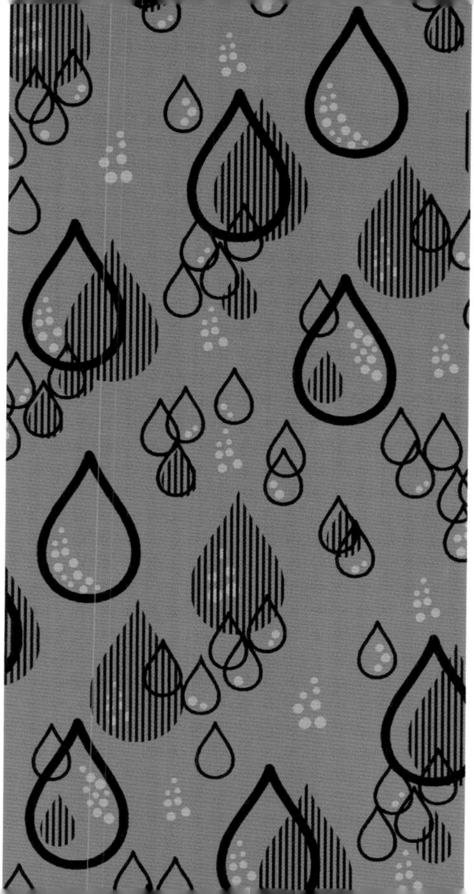

Nadja Girod (GER) www.nadjagirod.com

Manja Schiefer   (GER)   www.manjaschiefer.de

Christoph Ruprecht (GER) www.flywiththespaceship.com

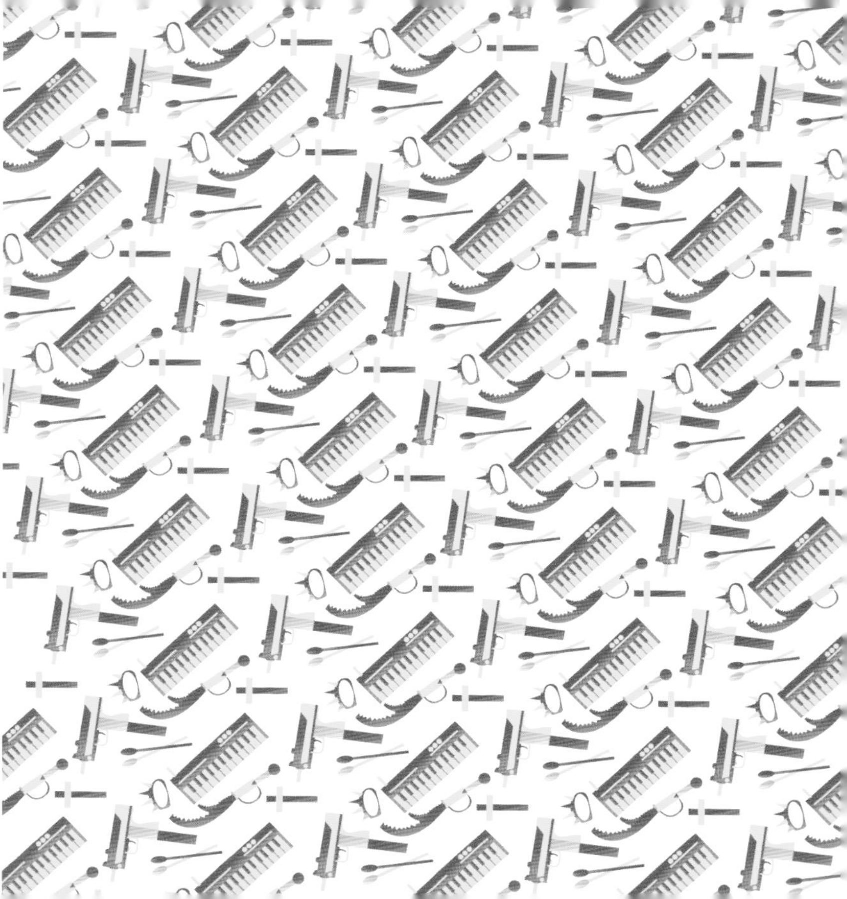

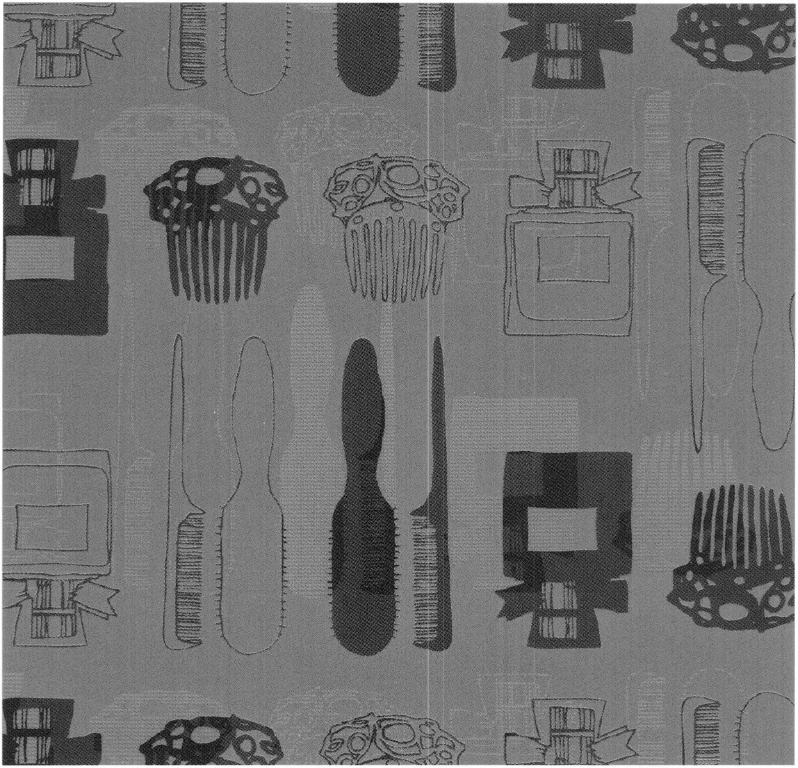

Janine Kunze (GER) www.myspace.de/nineapfelsine

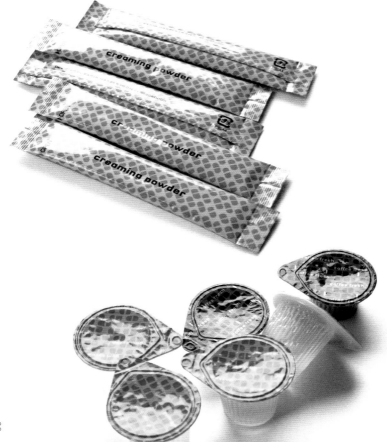

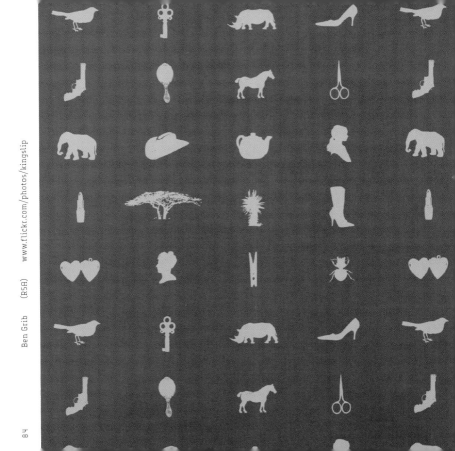

4. Unirvi il tritato di pollo,
le uova sbattute,
l'olio, il sale (abbondante)
e il pepe nero.

Kiri Coles (AUS) kiricoles@hotmail.com

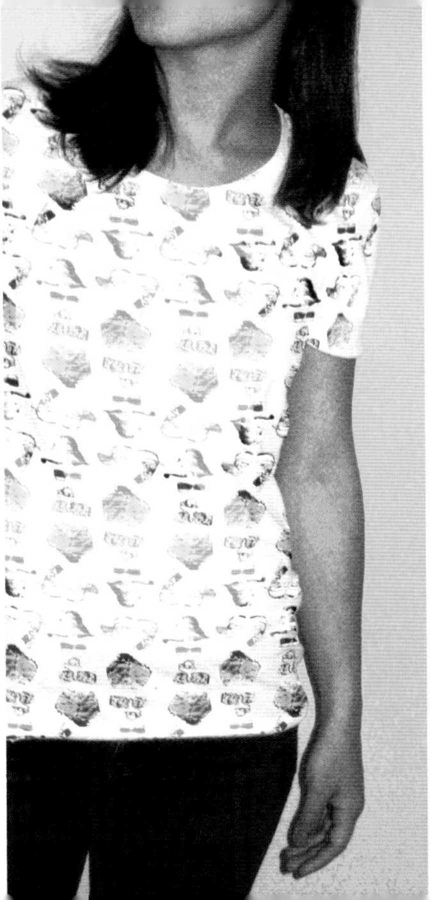

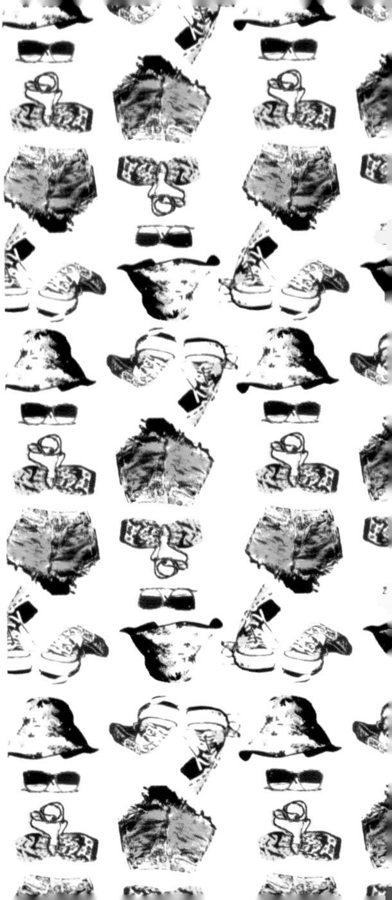

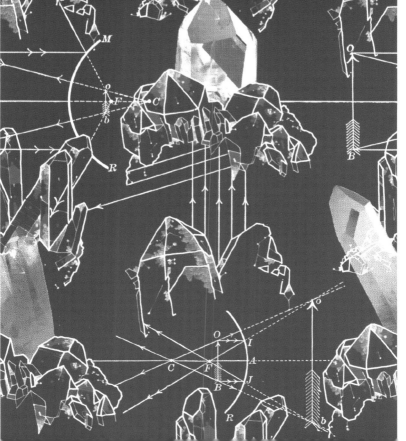

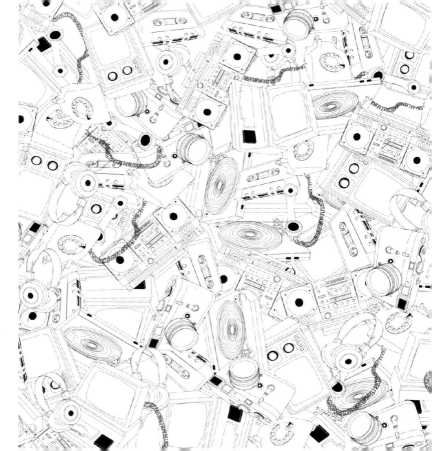

"red umbrellas
stop the rain"
and I am in **love** with **you**

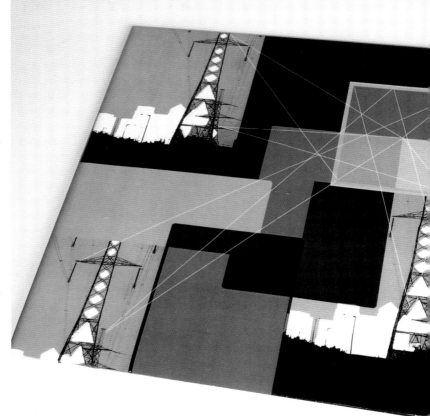

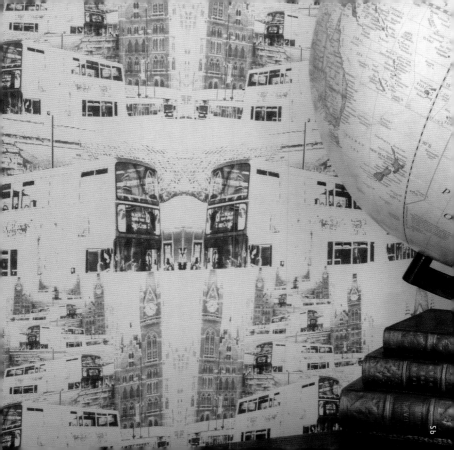

Aline Cardoso Rodrigues (BRA) www.tzdz.com.br

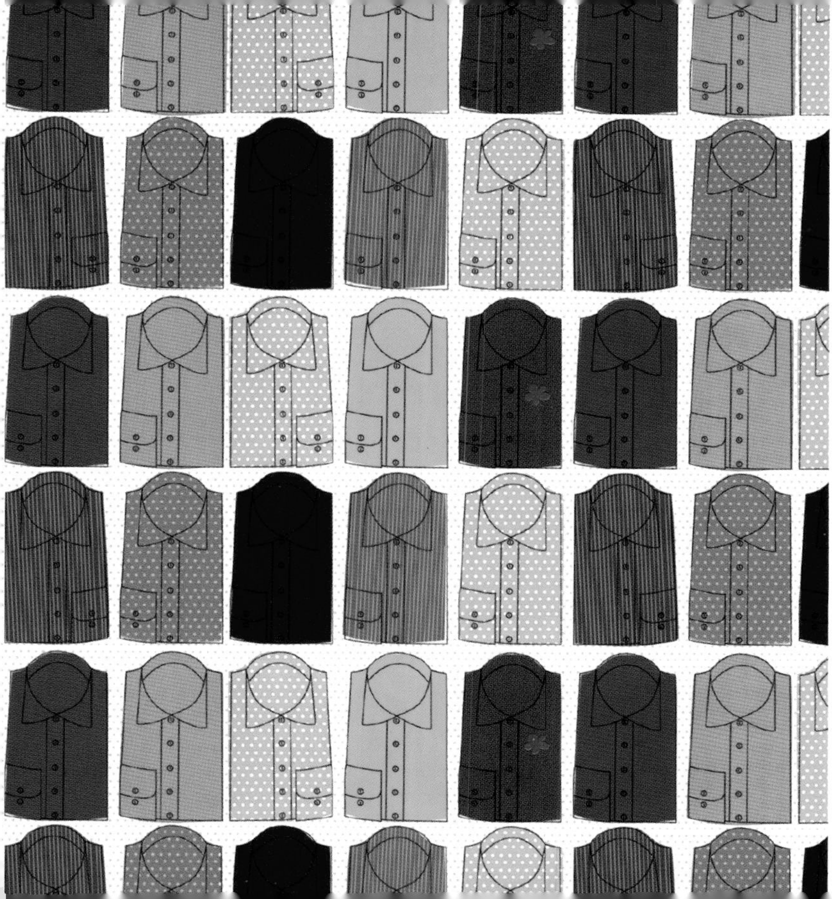

Kerstin Jacobmeyer (GER) puenktchendesign@web.de

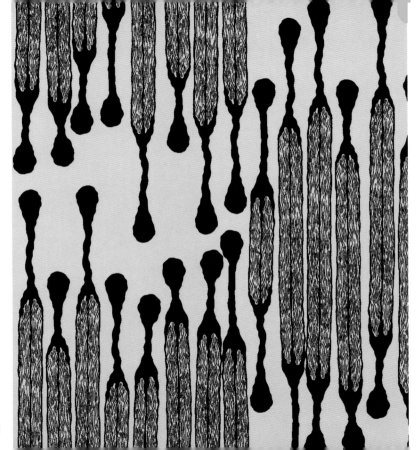

animals

dog, cat, bird, squirrel, wolf

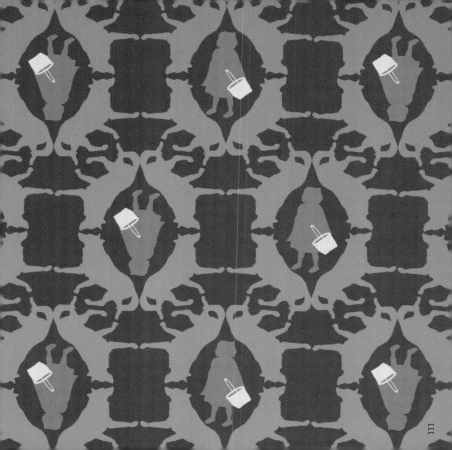

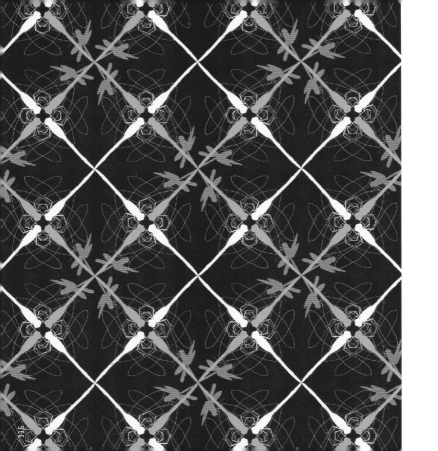

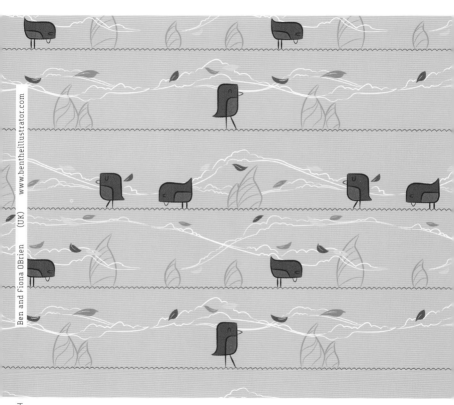

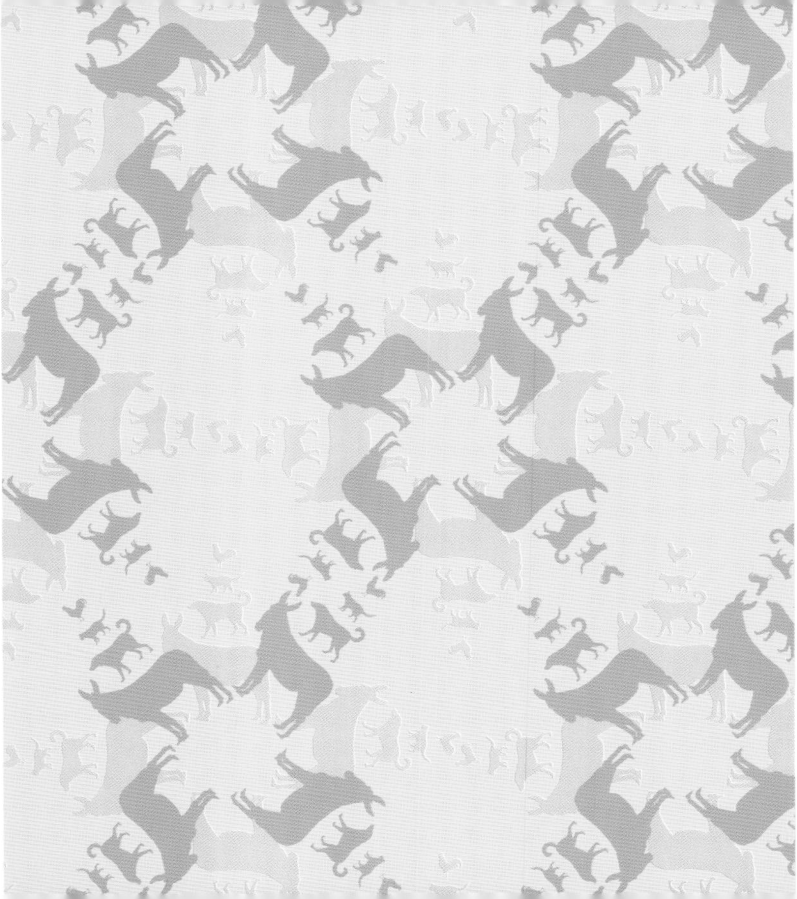

Olivier Arcioli (GER) www.olivier-jean-sebastian.com

Titus Leibing   (GER)   www.tituz.de

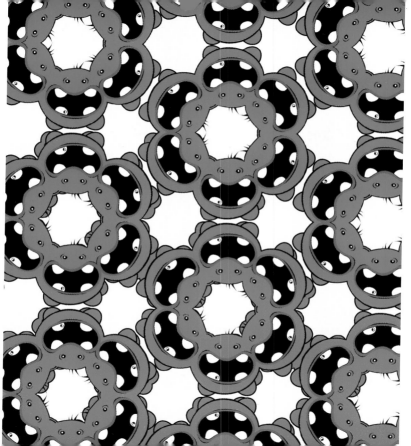

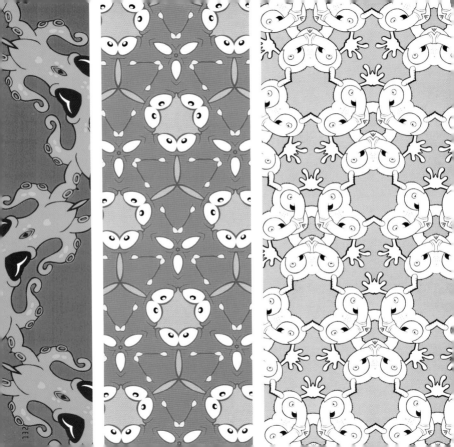

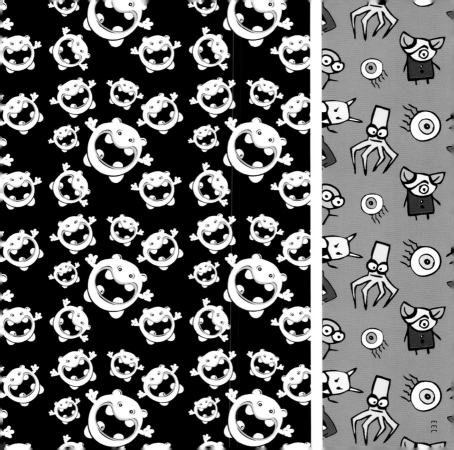

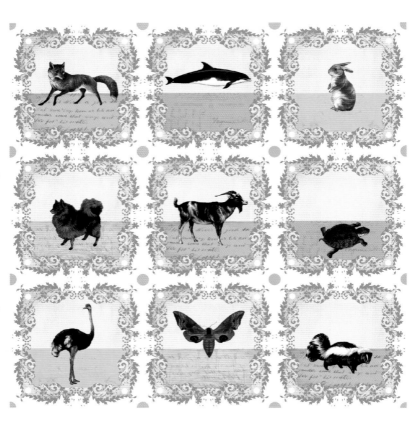

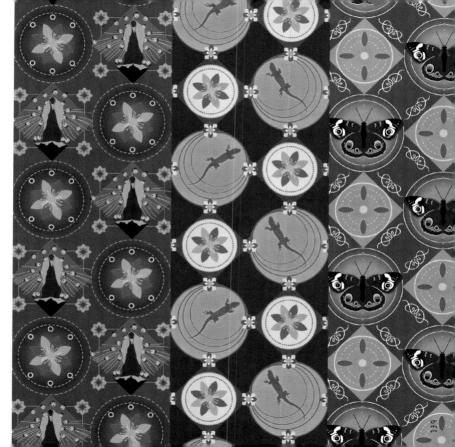

Carolyn Gavin   (CAN)   www.ecojot.com

Agnieszka Waczyńska   (POL)

154

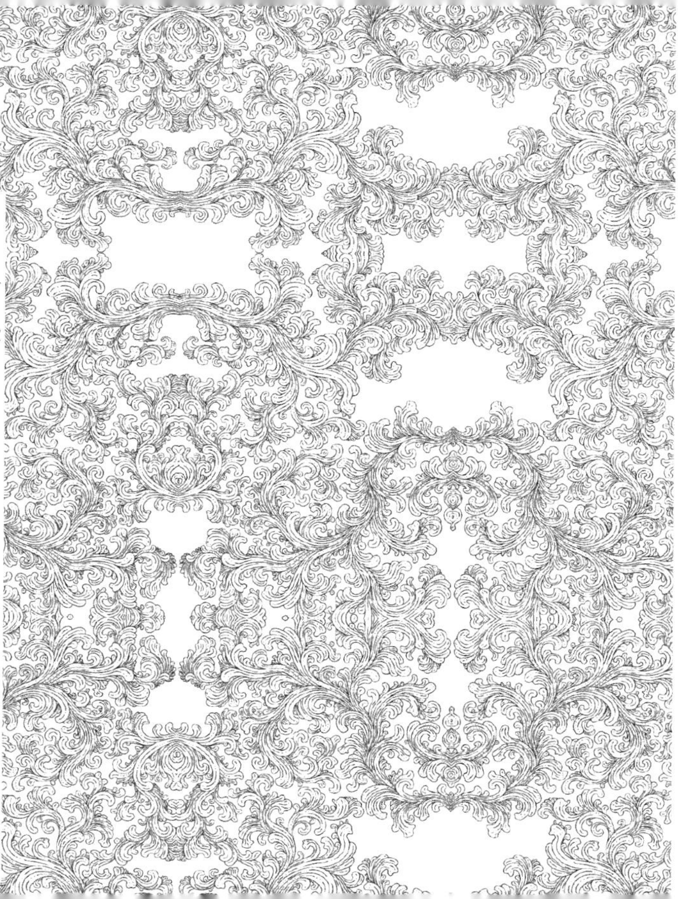

Lubov Malikova (UKR) www.flickr.com/photos/luba_ma

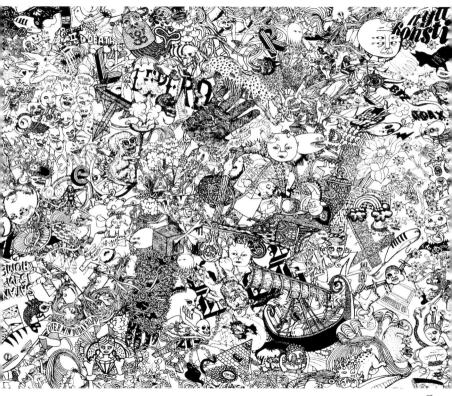

Lydia Meiying   (UK)   www.hellomeiying.com

Gemma Correll   (UK)   www.gemmacorrell.com

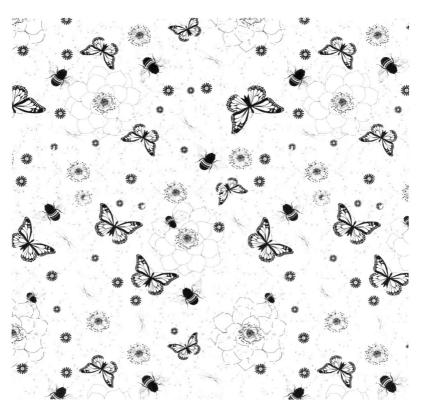

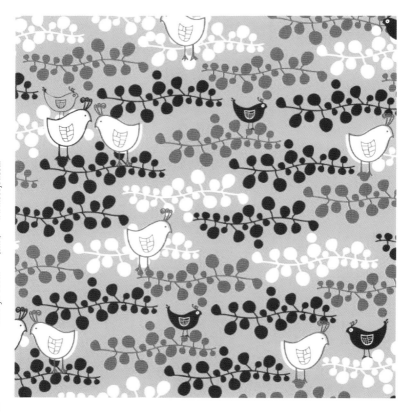

Swati Ahuja Gupta   (USA)

Sabine Reinhart (GER)   www.mynetty.de

Charlotte Warner   (UK)   charlottewarner@mac.com

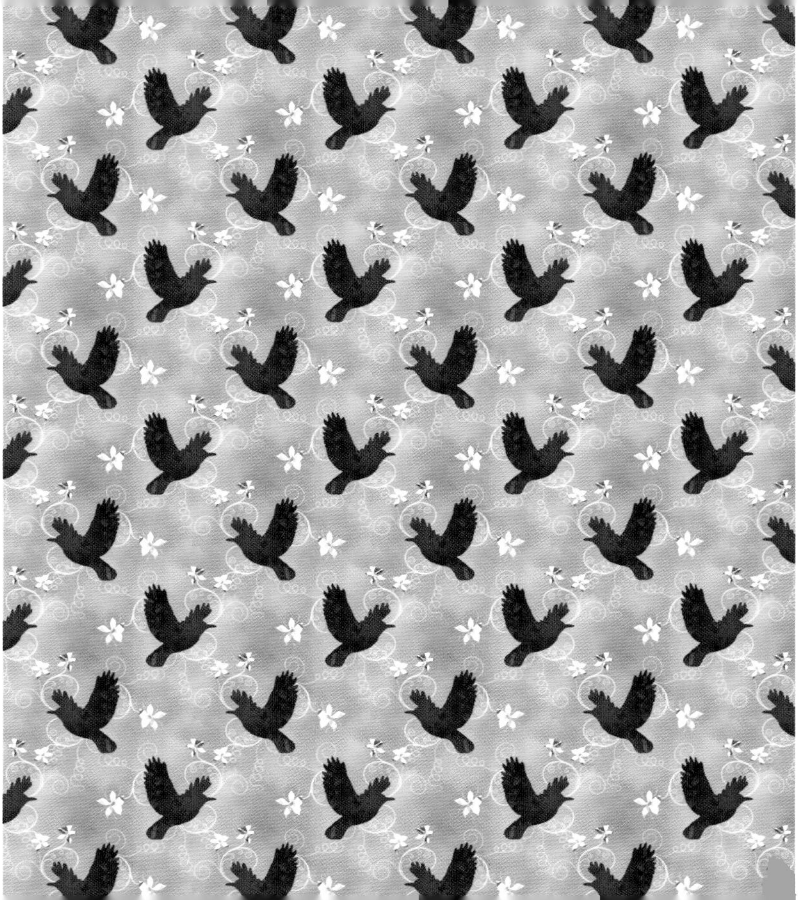

Sabine Reinhart (GER) www.patterrific.com

DOGMATA

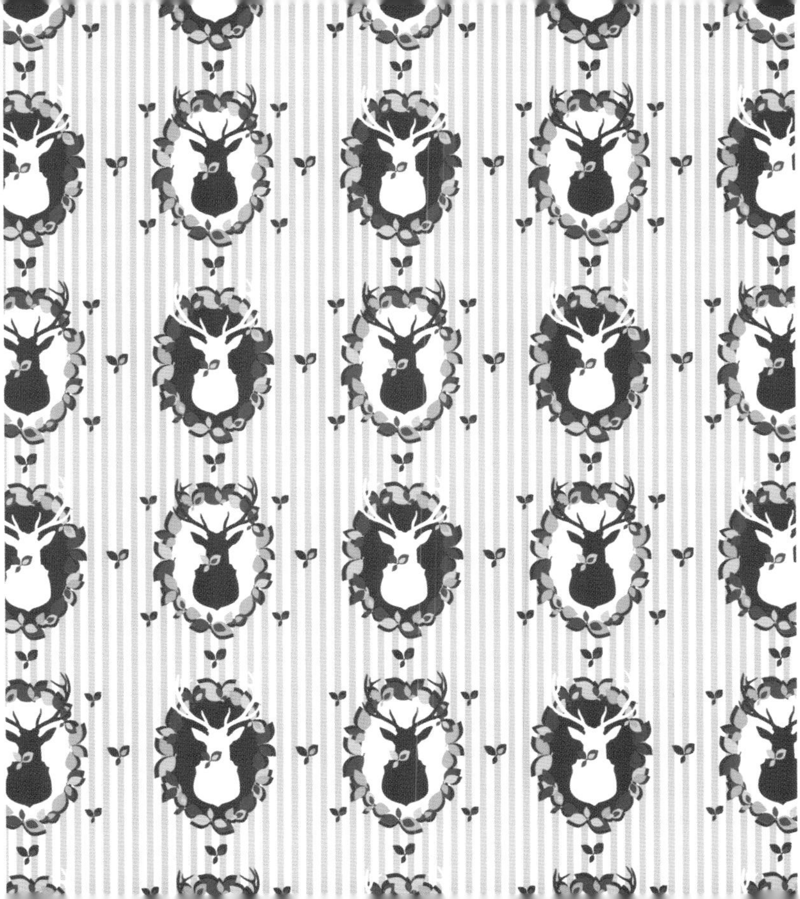

Lara Brehm (FRA) www.larabrehm.com

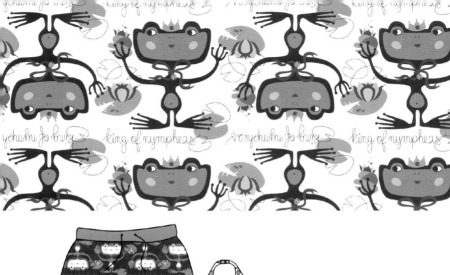

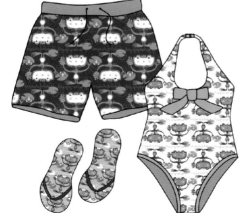

Jamie Oliver   (SUI)   www.schnuppe.ch

Ingo Walde   (GER)   www.einmalich.com

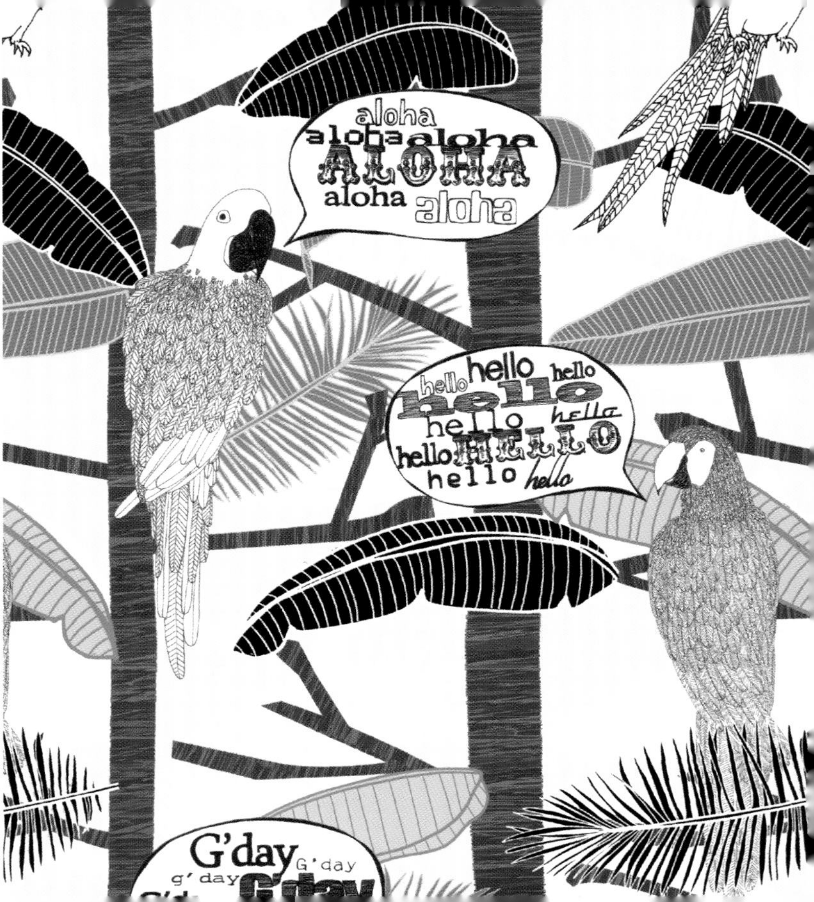

Lydia Meiying (UK) www.hellomeiying.com

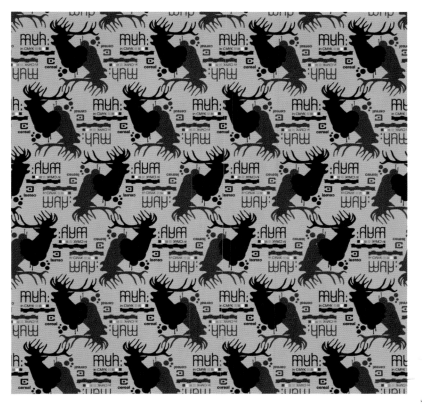

Jozef Vereš   (SLK)   www.4or.sk

Laurie

Christoph Ruprecht (GER)

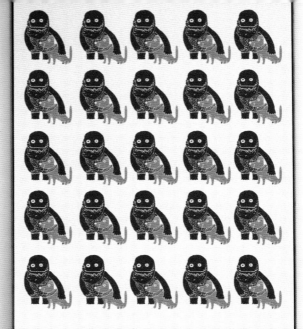

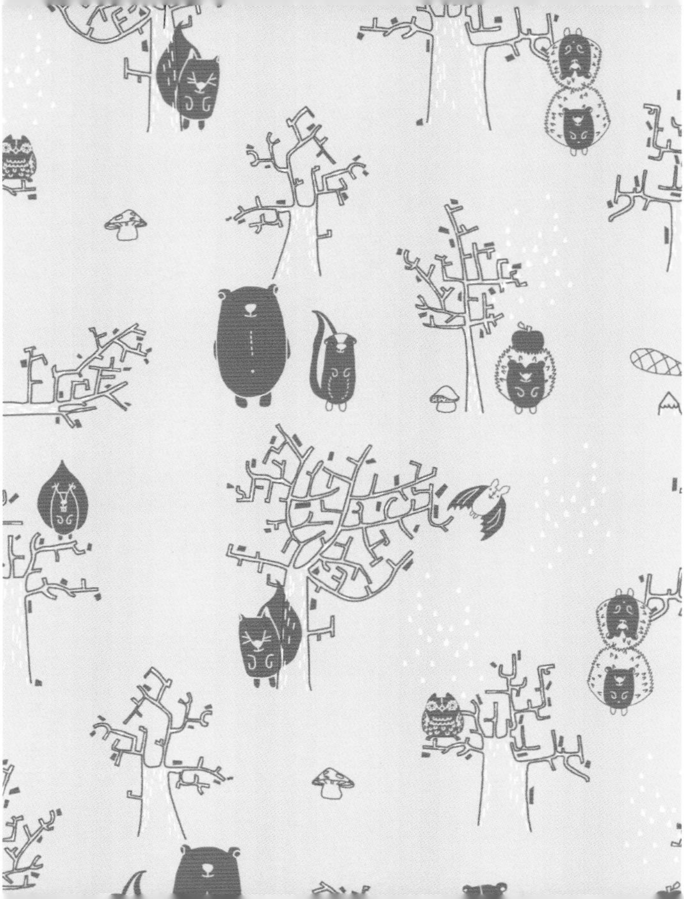

Agnieszka Waczyńska (POL) www.vaczor.art.pl

Katja Behre   (UK)   www.ellipopp.com

Aimee Wilder   (USA)

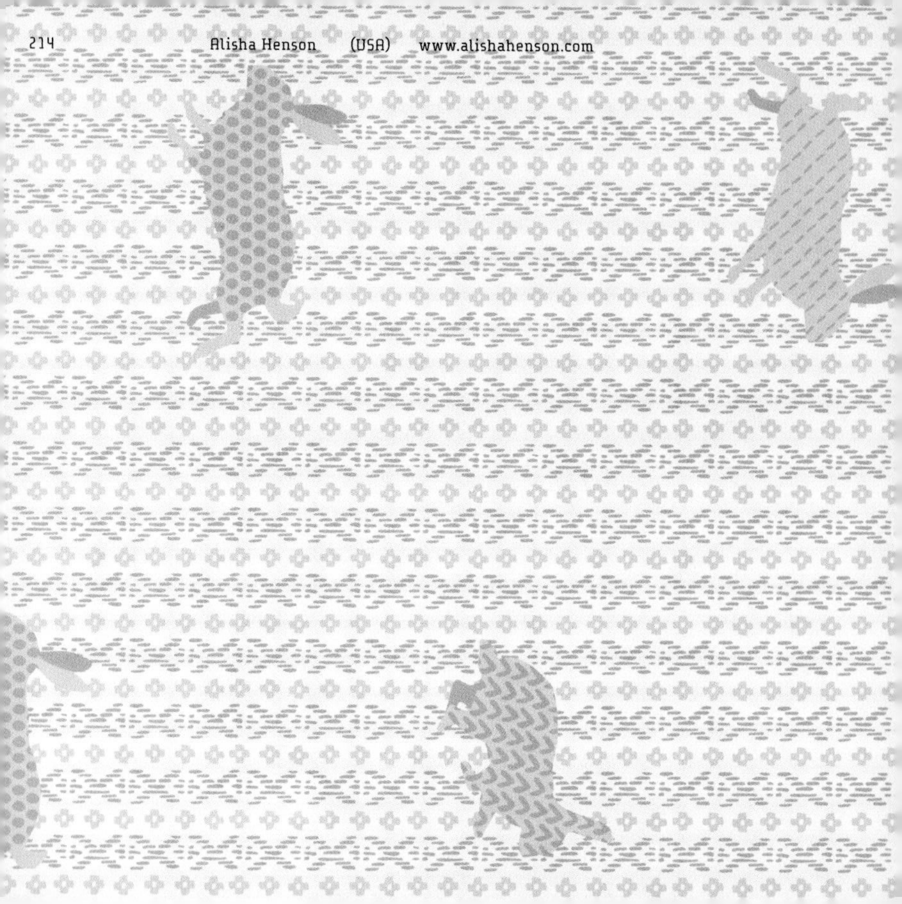

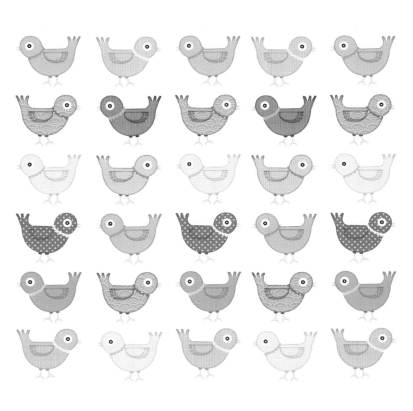

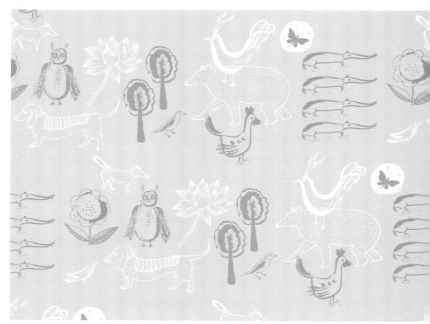

typo

number, word, text

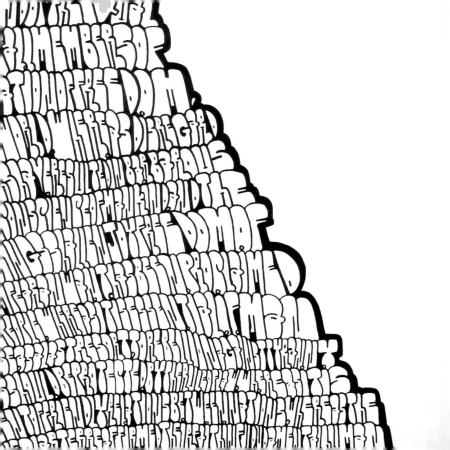

REVALER 10

nkfurter 10407 ✉

Allee ✉ Rykestr

✉ Pankow Karl

r Str. 23 Ⓢ Brees

EE Mauerpark Mü

Boxi⚷Winsst

tr. Liselotte-Herrmann-S

LEX ◄◄ 10407 Ama

www.smil.biz 🚗 🐕

rk REVALER 10
Frankfurter 10407
36 Allee Rykest
e Pankow Kar
Bree
rer Str. 23 S
LEE Mauerpark M
ark Boxi Winss
-Str. Liselotte-Herrmann-
ALEX 10407 Am
www.smil.biz

HADANEFTER FLYGER JAG OFTAST

WORSE. IF ONLY I COULD HAVE MORE SOME

I TOOK ALL OF THEM AND FELT STRANGE AND

THEM AND THEY SAID I WOULD MAKE ME BETTER

Me to eat

hey told EYES EYES EYES

G MER ATT GRÅU BUSSEN

DOM HAR hittat

KAN DET VARA SÅ LÄNGE. JAG

HAN ÄR PÅ VÄG?

ÖSTEN HAR MÖGLAT I KYLEN

NOT put

ICE THEM UNTIL IT IS

NEJ, INTE I ANSIKTET

HIMSELF

35 ST

Aus ihr en...
er aus, und zu...

Rémy Zaugg

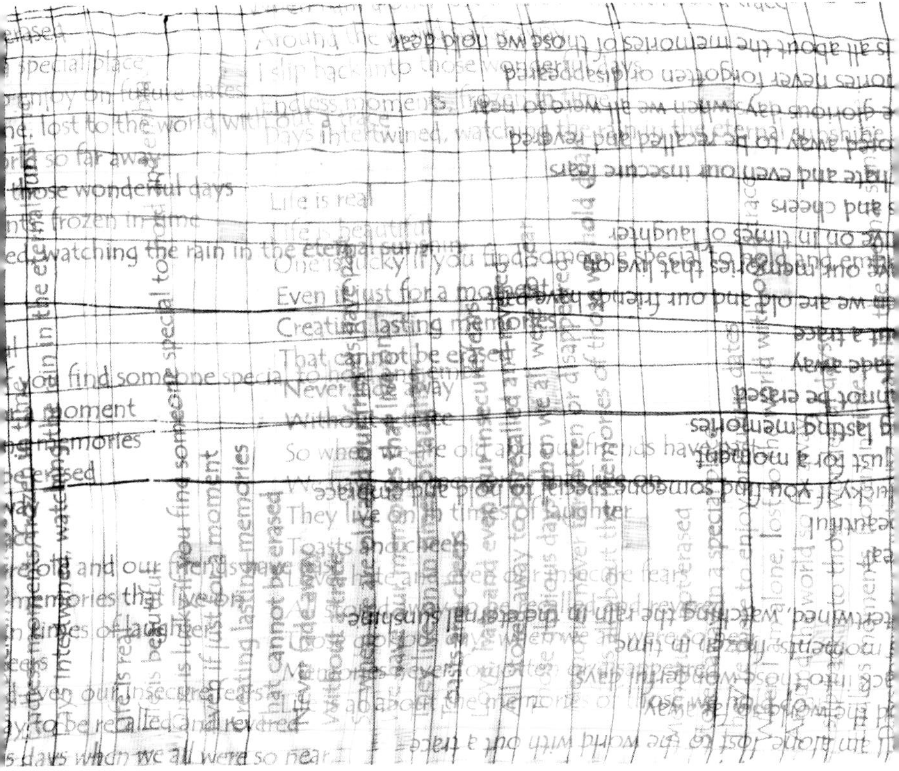

Ekaterina Kurochkina (GER) tkanikurik@yahoo.com

Rachel Holmes   (UK)

www.behance.net/Rachel_holmes

INFORMATION

info

PAYPOINTS

OXENTS

EX in A book that YOU WANT HELP DI

SEEK AD! refere

Exchanging locate

ites Purchase buy

itm ASK fl you

HAPPY

TO INF RECOM

HELP! ENDAT

where Assis

Can you help find a che

me? GIFTS KO

let u

80 million children in the world do not go to school and live in immense poverty. We want to give these children a chance to create a better life for themselves. Ask at the information point for further details.

RESOURCE

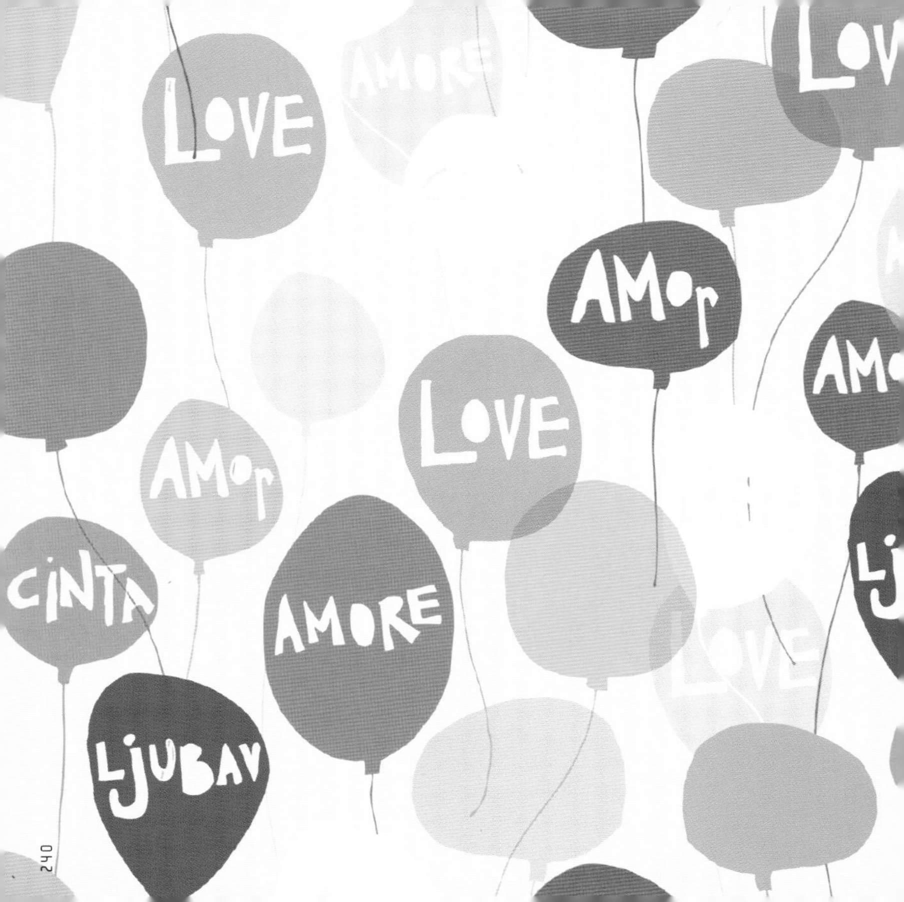
LOVE
AMORE
AMOr
LOVE
AMOr
CINTA
AMORE
LOVE
LJUBAV

human

people, face, body

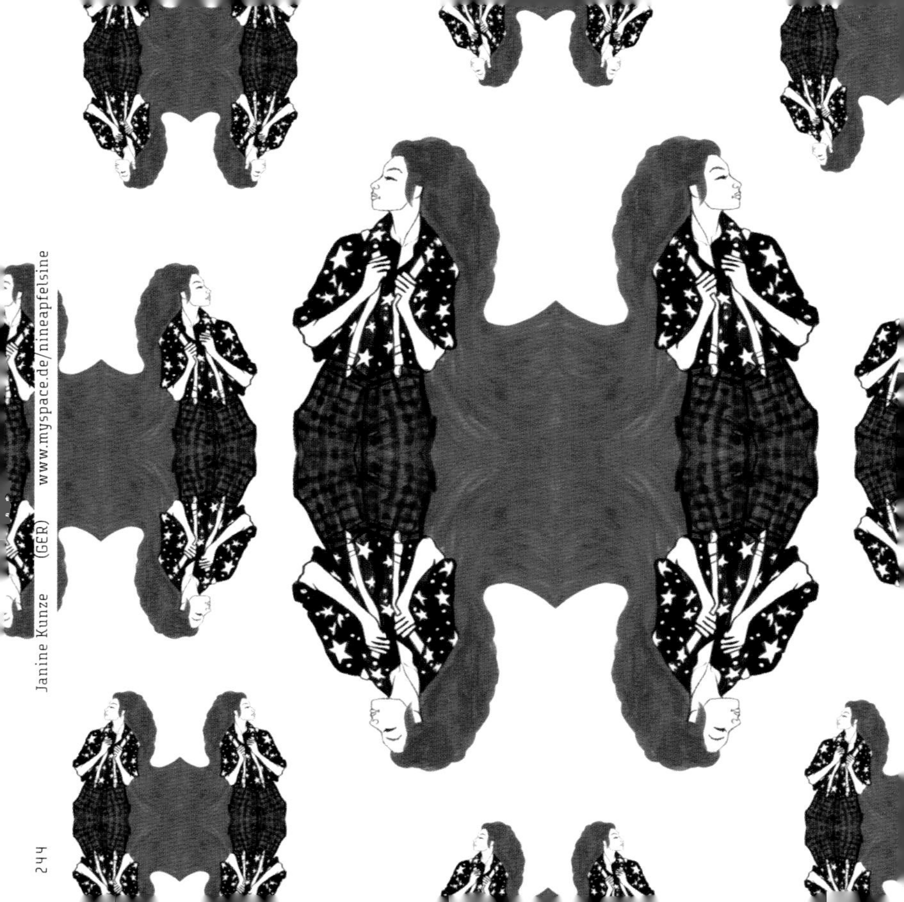

Janine Kunze (GER) www.myspace.de/nineapfelsine

Sarah Knorr (GER)

www.sarahs-safari.de

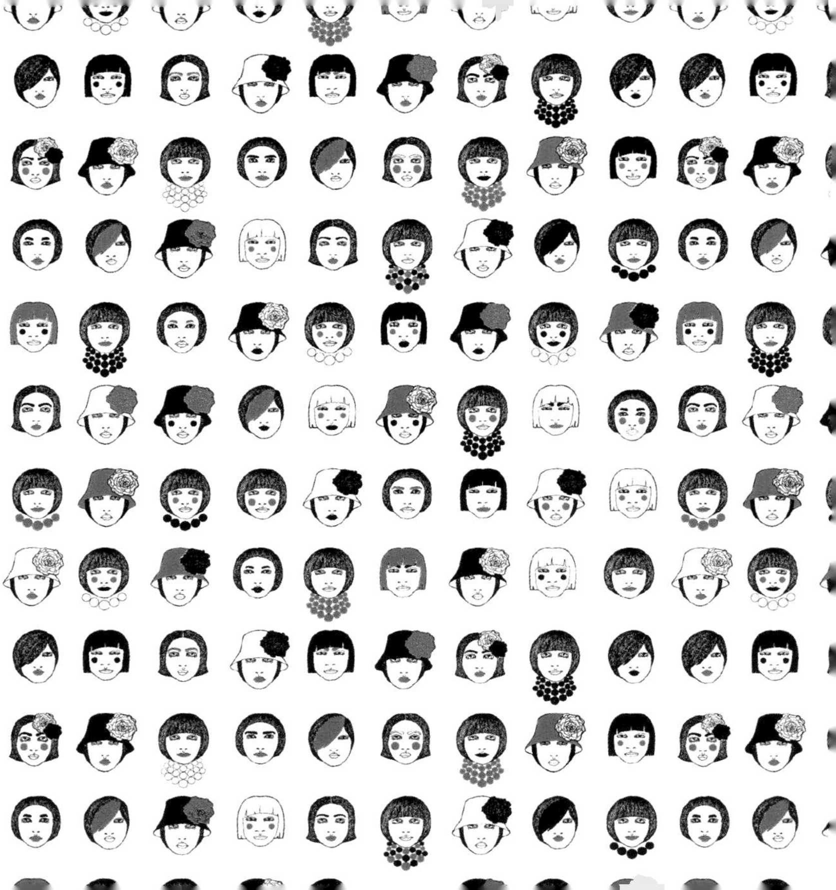

Lubov Malikova (UKR) www.flickr.com/photos/luba_ma

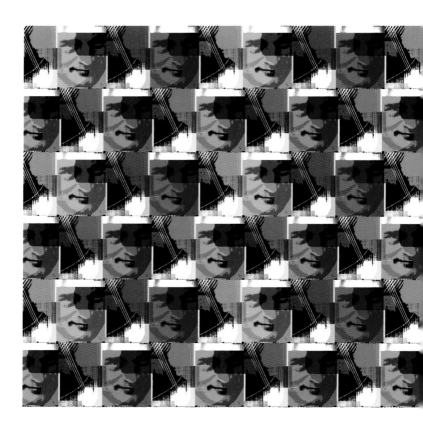

Isabelle Kunz (SUI) www.troismiettes.com

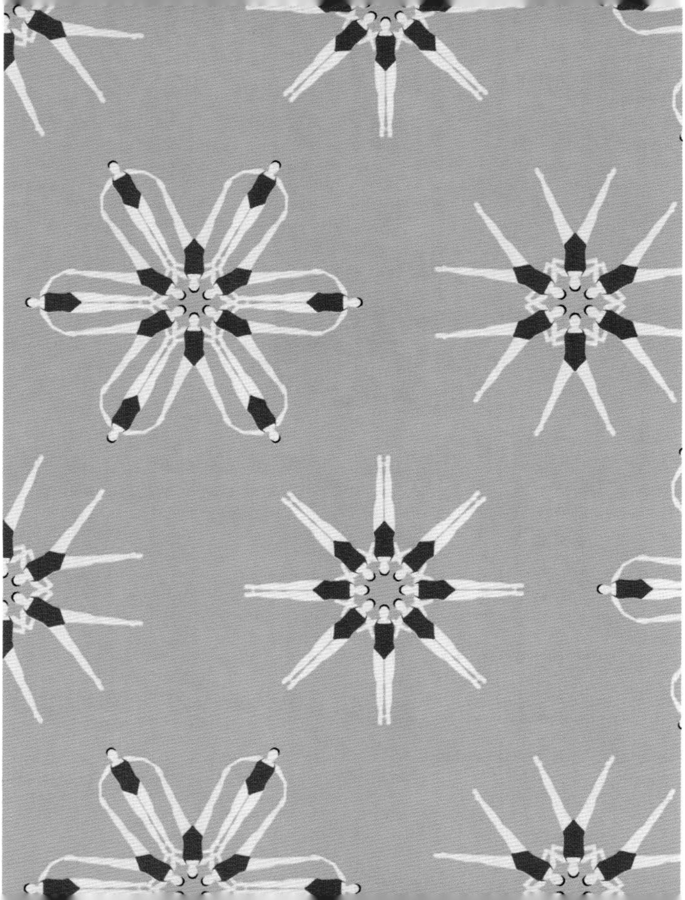

Olivier Arcioli   (GER)   www.olivier-jean-sebastian.com

Julia Rothman   (USA)   www.juliarothman.com

Christian Schaarschmidt   (GER)   www.illunatic.de

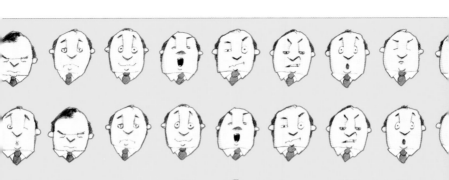

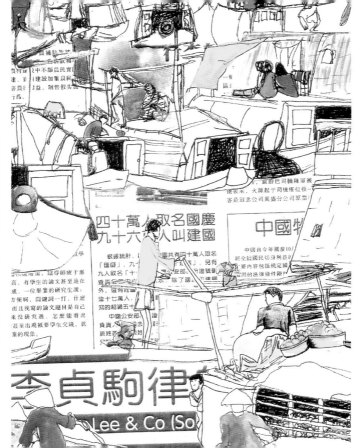

Stefanie Axmann   (GER)   www.stefanieaxmann.com

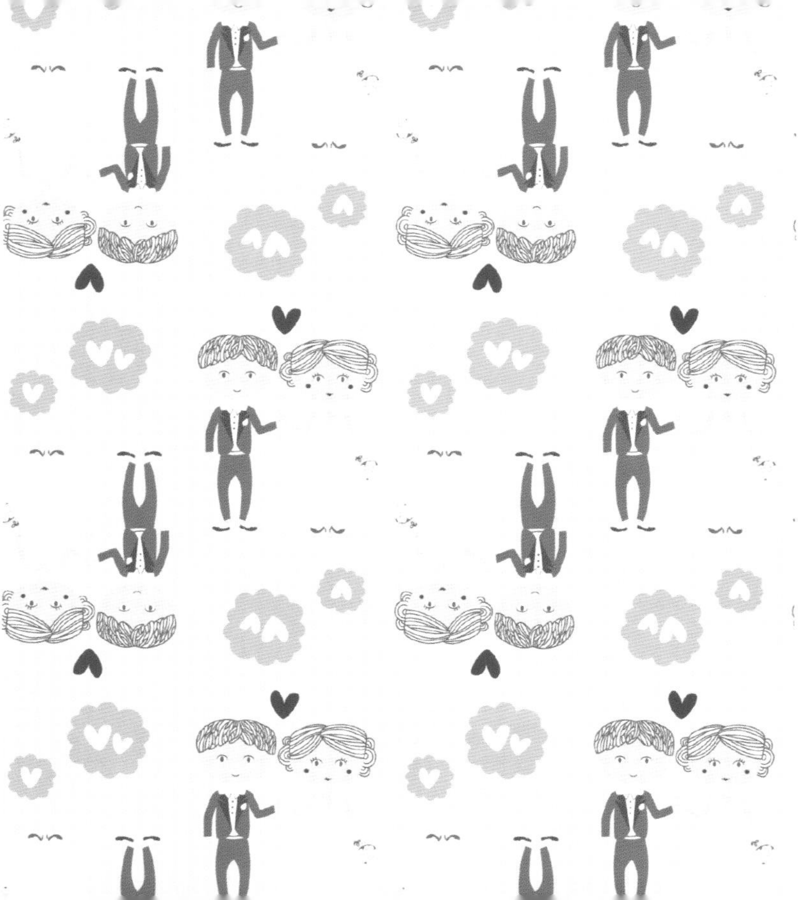

Lara Brehm (FRA) www.larabrehm.com

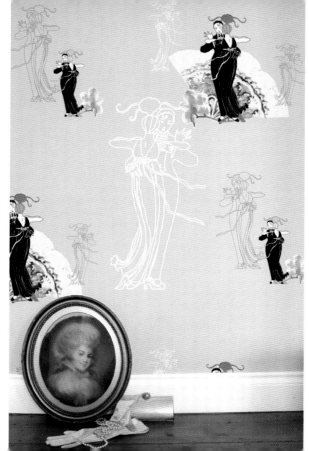

Katja Behre   (UK)   www.ellipopp.com

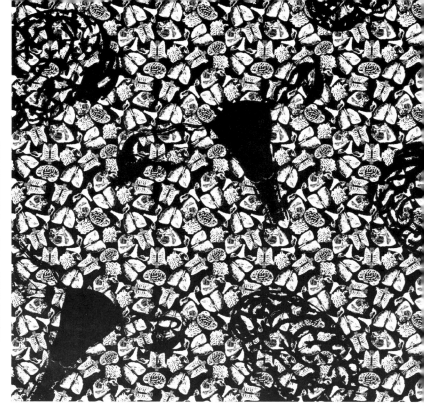

Lubov Malikova (UKR) www.flickr.com/photos/luba_ma

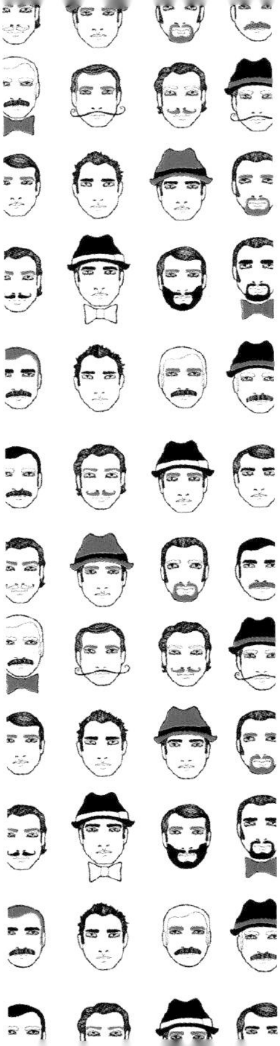

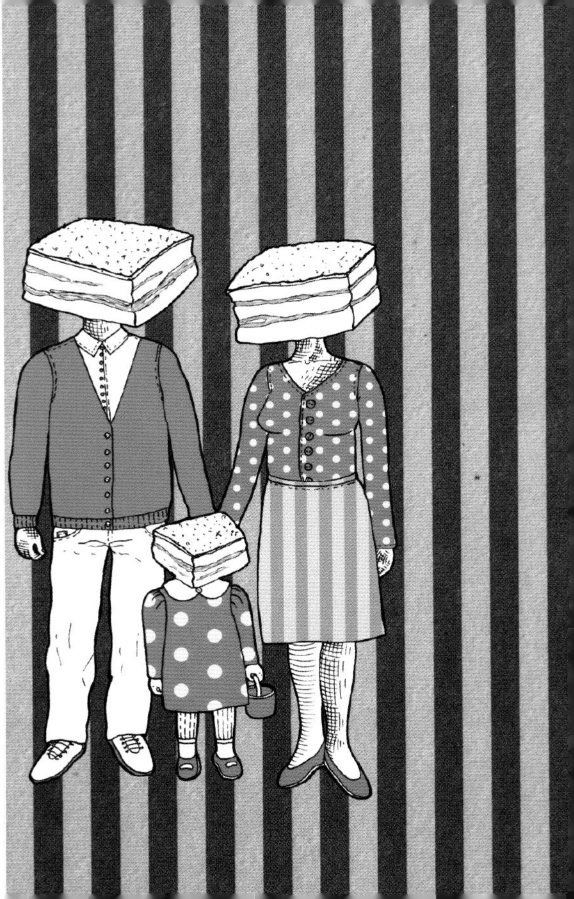

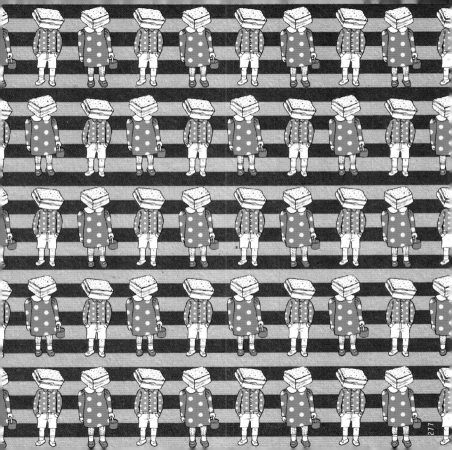

luhuert@gmail.com

(ESP)

Marina Huertas

Janine Kunze (GER) www.myspace.de/nineapfelsine

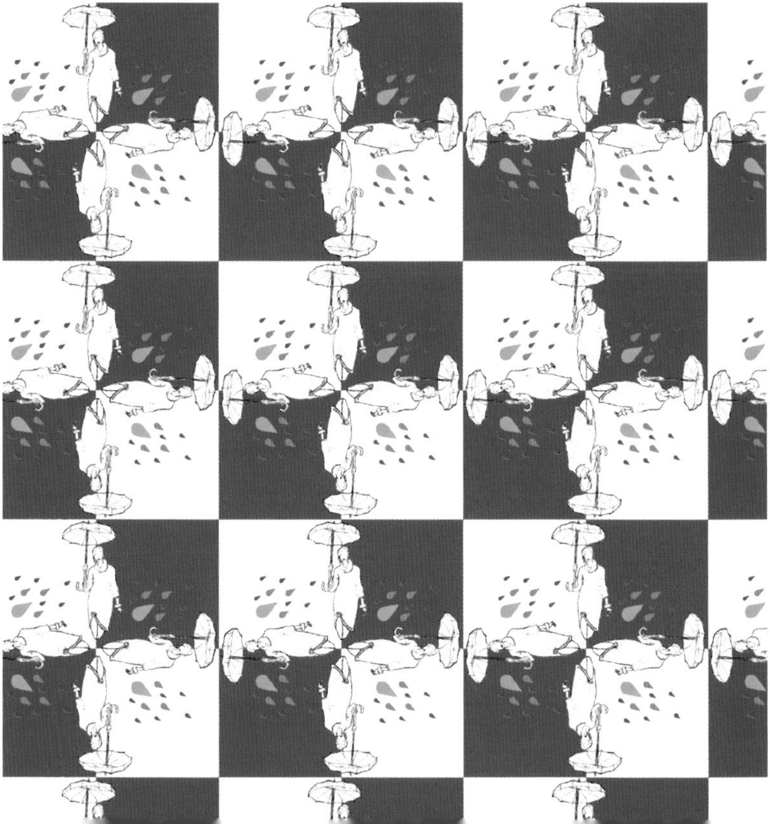

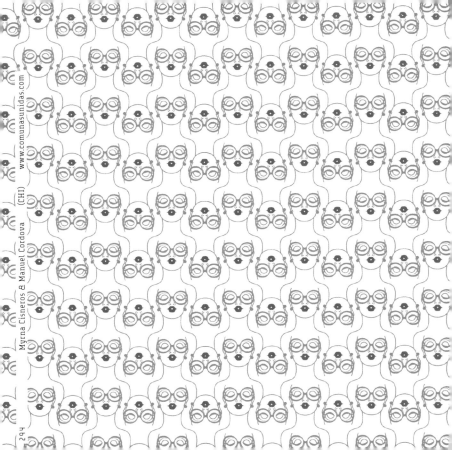

www.sailthouforth.com

(USA)

Catherine A. Kane

geometric

circle, line, square,
surface, point

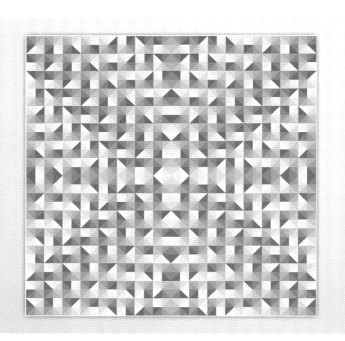

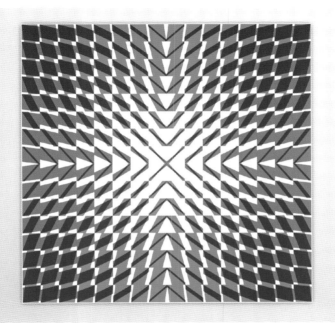

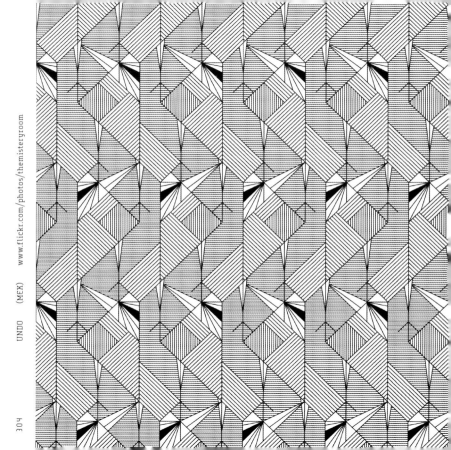

304

POUDRE deRIZ

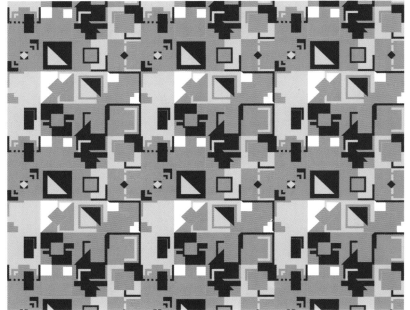

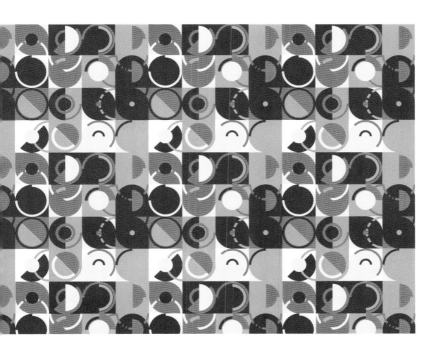

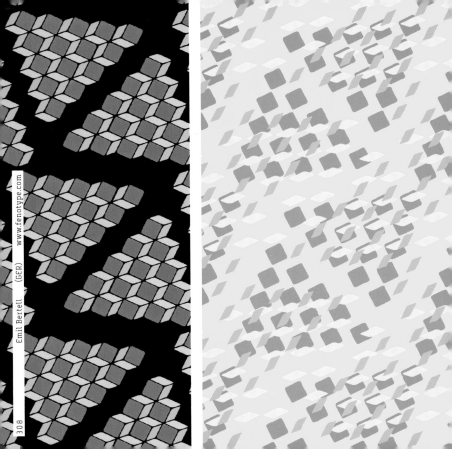

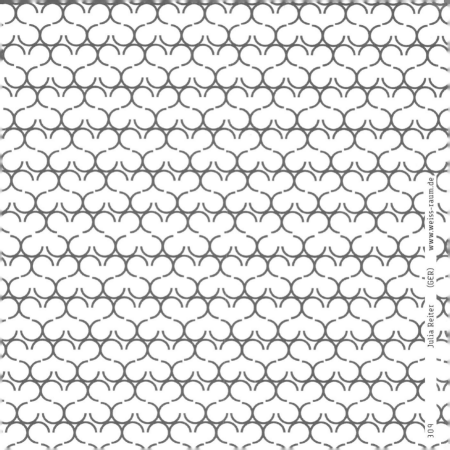

www.weiss-raum.de

(GER)

Julia Reiter

309

Ana Montiel   (ESP)

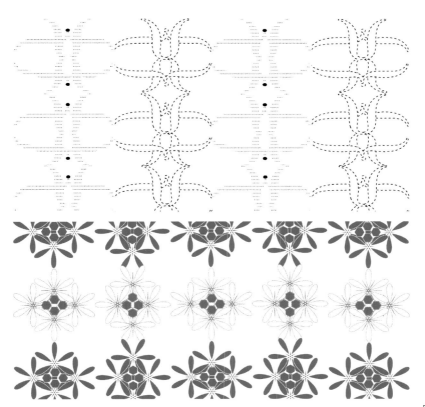

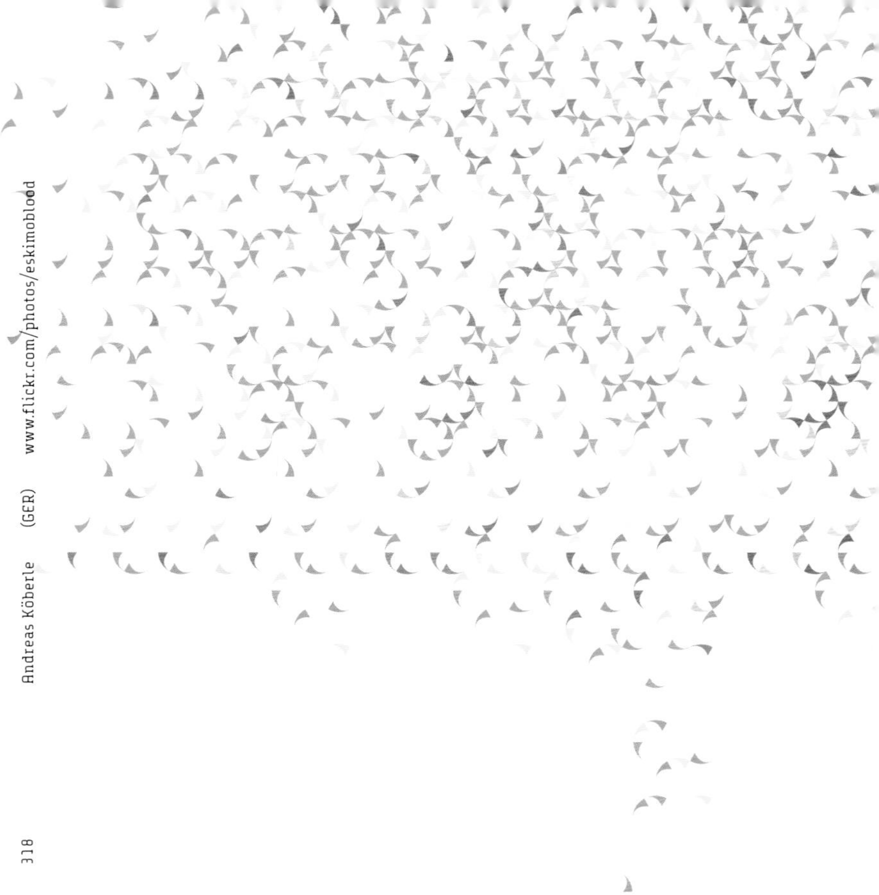

Andreas Köberle (GER) www.flickr.com/photos/eskimoblood

Martina Wagner   (GER)   www.ggg-nw.de

HUMULUS LUPULUS / LUBET / LÚPULO / LÚPALO
FLOR ENTERA
herbarium
kuasia
kuassia amara l.
QUASSIA AMARA L/ KUASSIA AMARA / QUASIA / IÑARR
200 GR
RoSella
papaveR Rhoeas L
herbarium
PAPAVER RHOEAS L. / ROSELLA / AMAPOLA / LOBEDAR
HOJA ENTERA

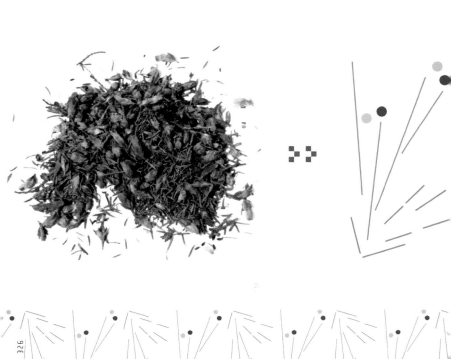

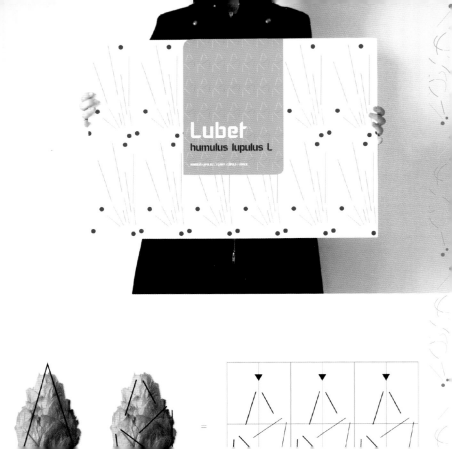

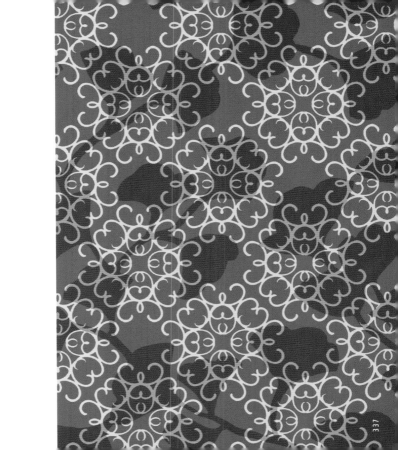

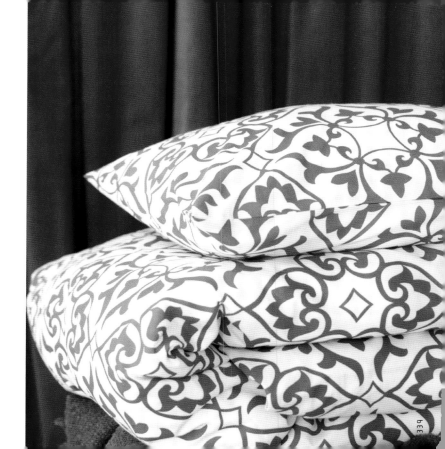

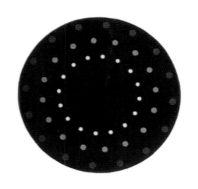

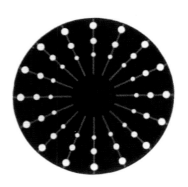

343

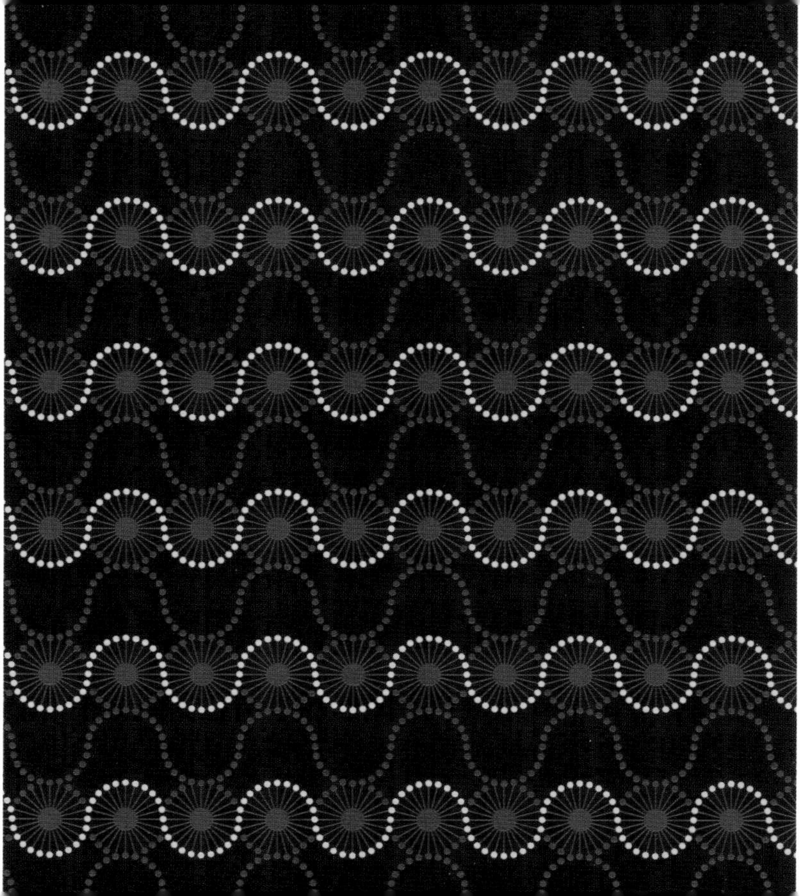

 Caroline Wall (UK) www.carolinewalldesign.co.uk

www.sgreendesigns.com

Sarah Green   (USA)

345

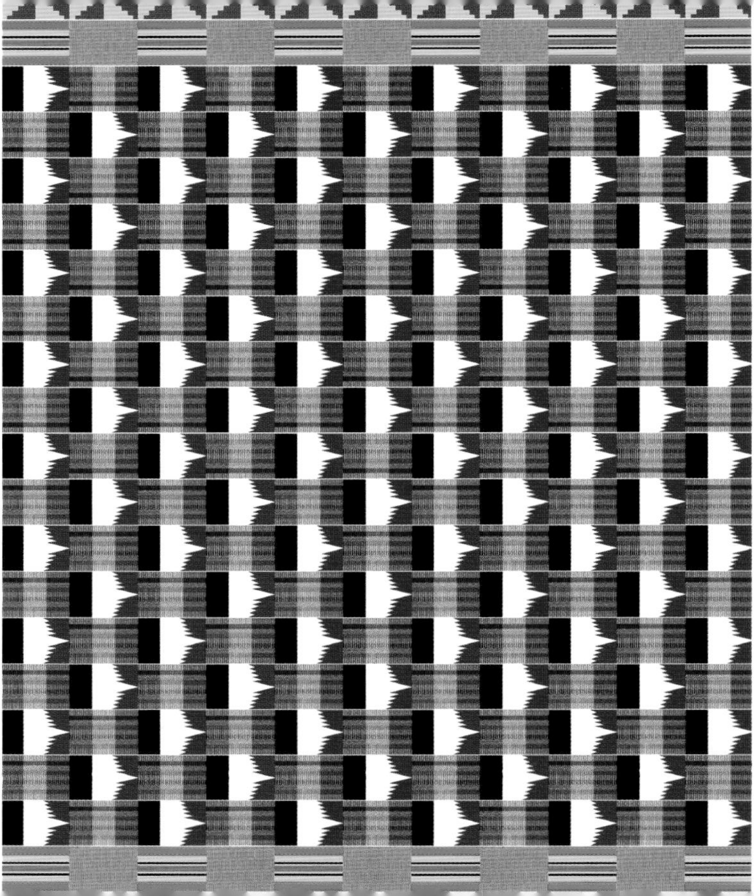

Aaron V. Mobley (USA) www.flickr.com/photos/avmobley

Liesa Rustler (GER) liesa.rustler@gmx.de

musterbeispiele

erstellt von liesa rustler

David Matthew Parker (USA) www.flickr.com/photos/vividp

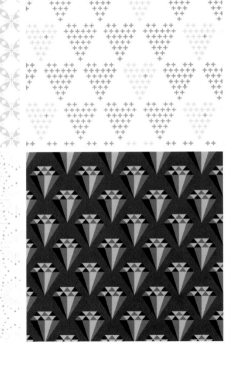

Martina Wagner   (GER)

Goh Tze Yee (MAS) tyee_10@yahoo.com

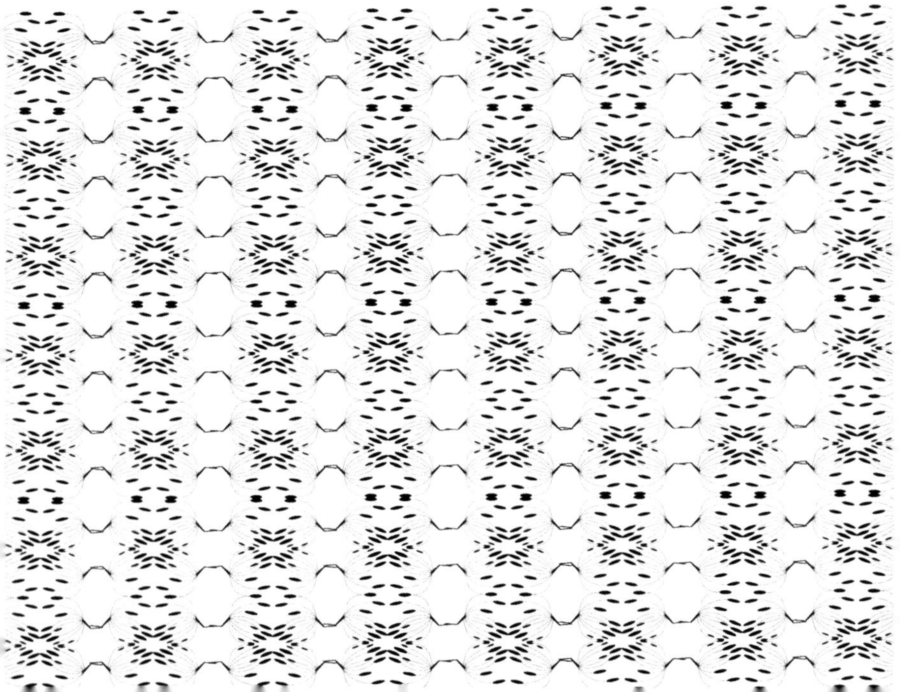

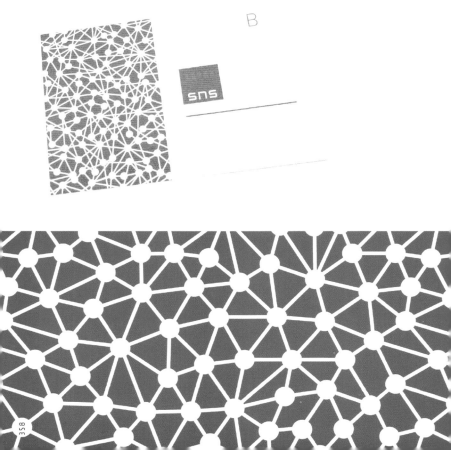

B

sns

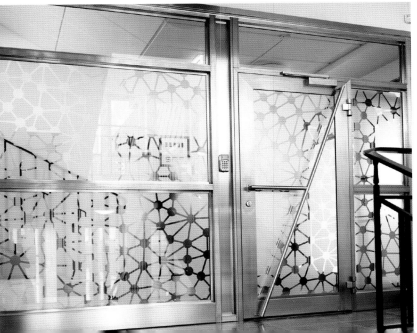

Karin Hagelström (SWE) www.hagelstromdesign.se

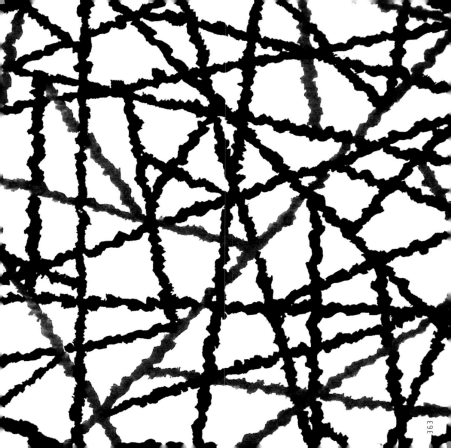

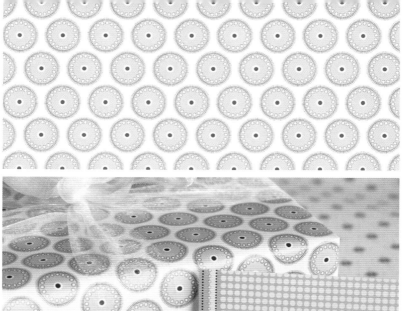

Viel Glück

www.mynetty.de

Sabine Reinhart   (GER)

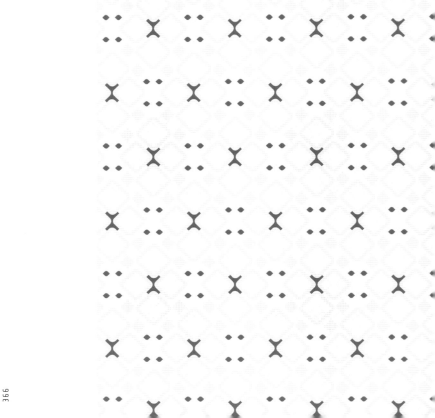

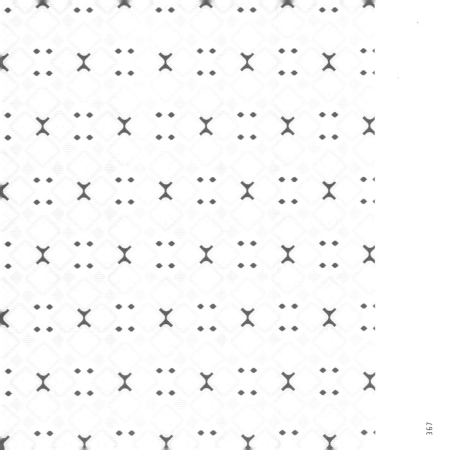

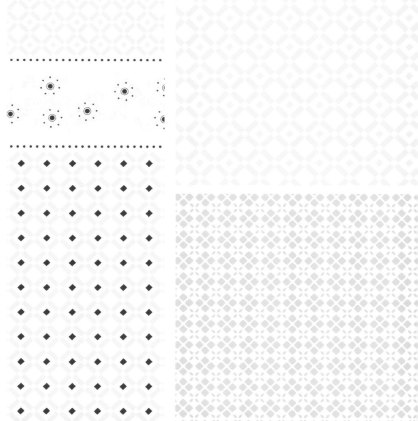

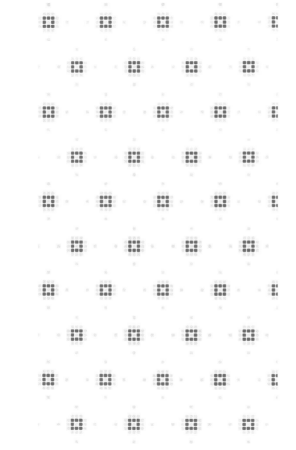

371

Mareike Hadeler   (GER)   www.mareiki.de

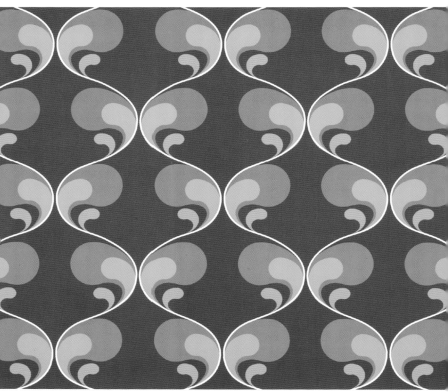

Natalie Singh   (UK)   natalie@artisticvisions.co.uk

Meyke Link   (HOL)

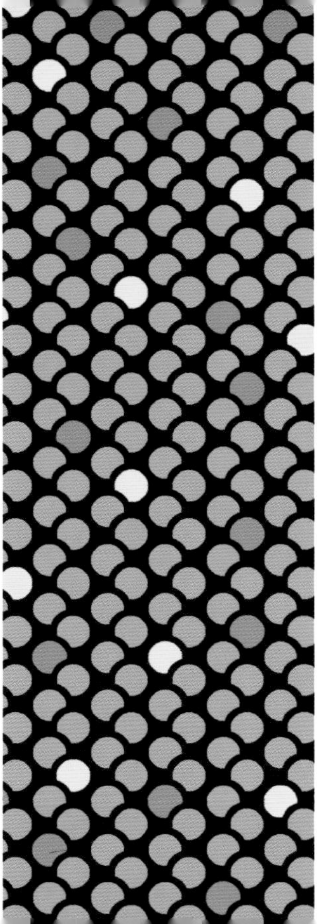

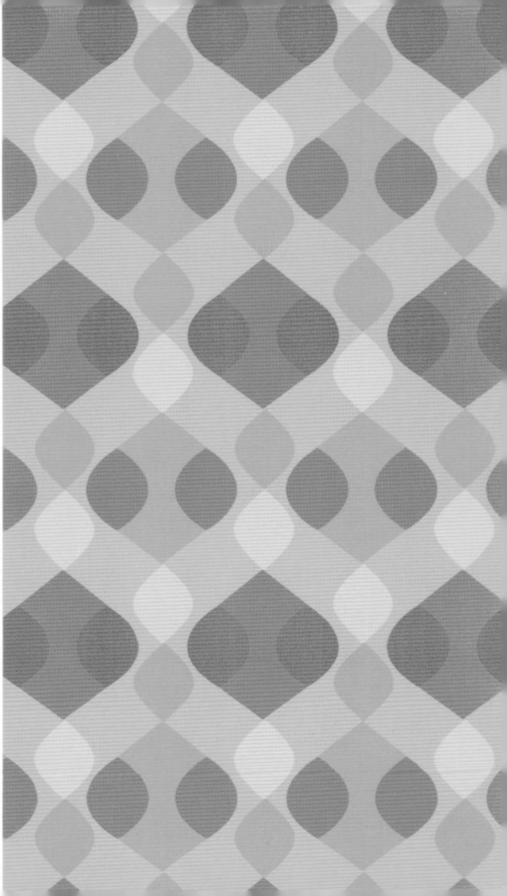

Nadja Girod (GER) www.nadjagirod.com

Cristina Bocaranda Belisario   (USA)

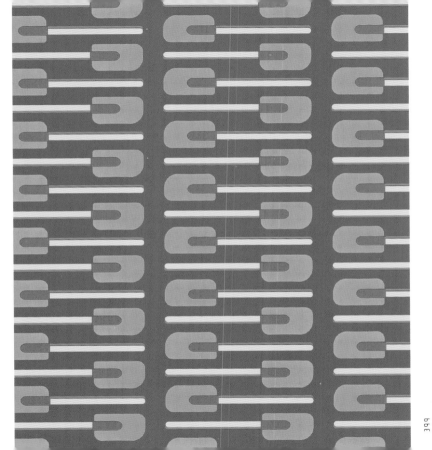

Andreas Köberle   (GER)

408

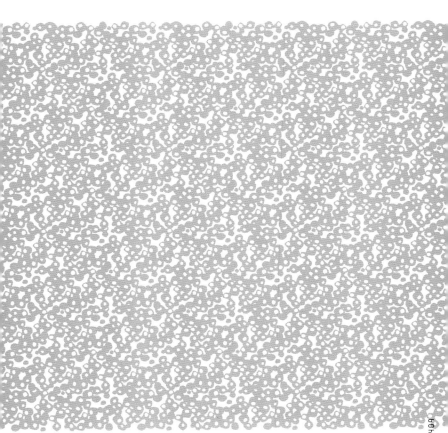

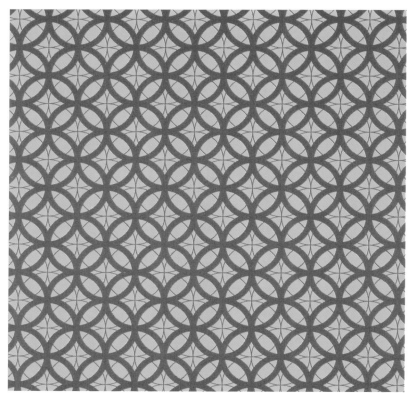

Sandra Praun   (SWE)

410

Michel M.   (GER)

(POR)

Ana Romero Monteiro

413

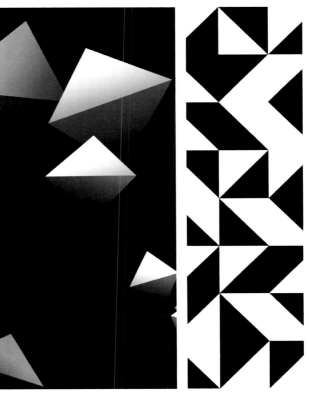

Eike Mitte   (GER)   www.vectorian.de

415

Katja Behre   (UK)   www.elitpopp.com

Annette Taylor-Anderson   (UK)   www.atadesigns.com

417

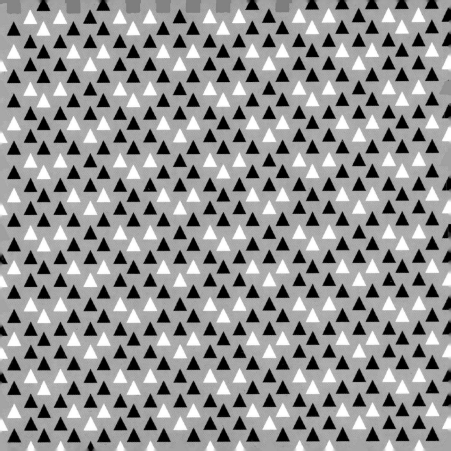

Jan Slovak   (CZE)

Vladimir Smokov   (CZE)

428

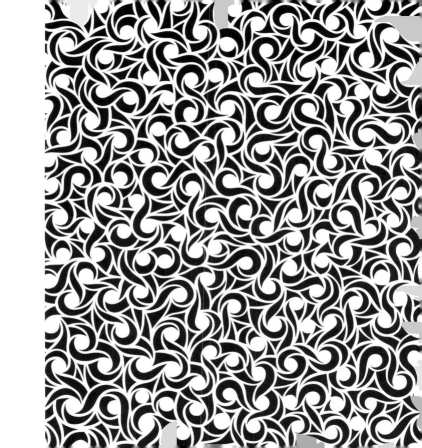

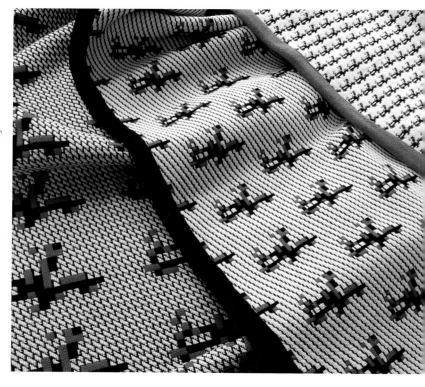

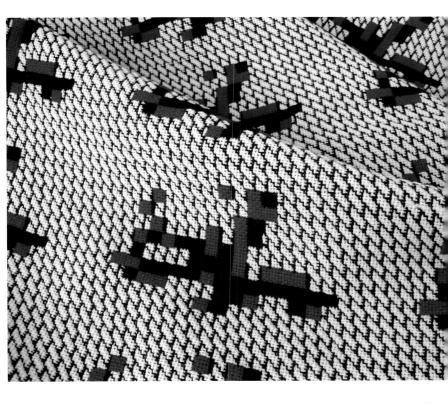

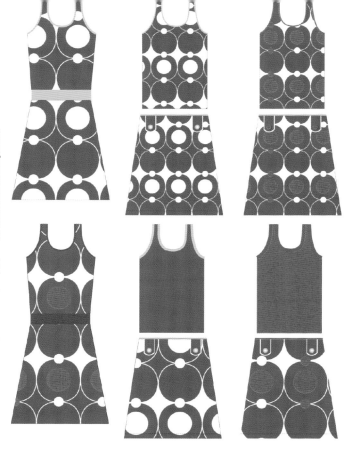

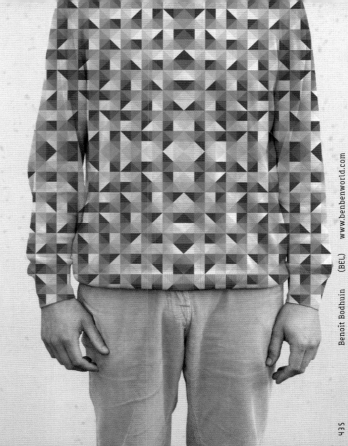

Benoit Bodhuin   (BEL)   www.benbenworld.com

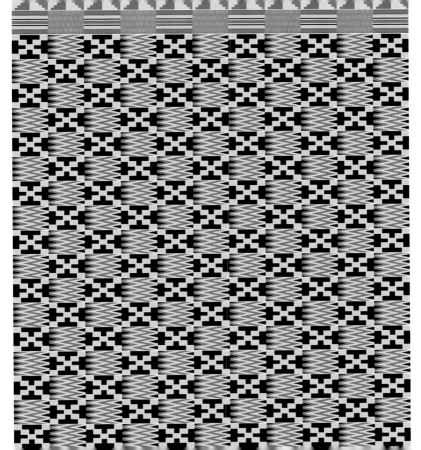

437

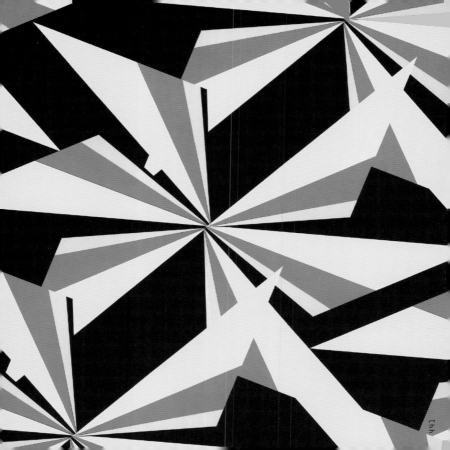

abstract

psychedelic, unreal,
insubstantial

Pomme Chan   (UK)   www.pommepomme.com

Lust for Loot

446

Lenka Petzold   (GER)   info@lenkapetzold.de

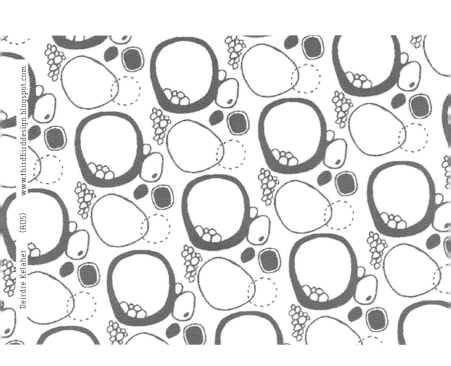

Von Glitschka   (USA)   www.glitschka.com

Julia Reiter   (GER)

456

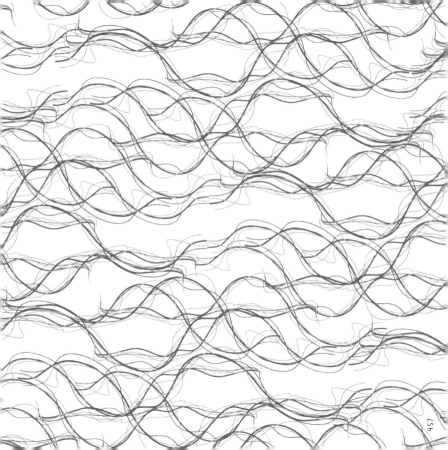

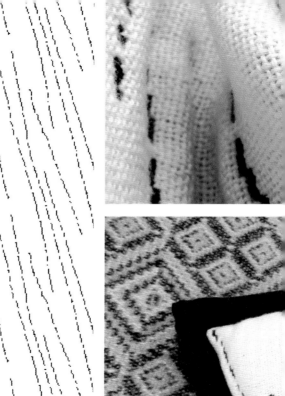

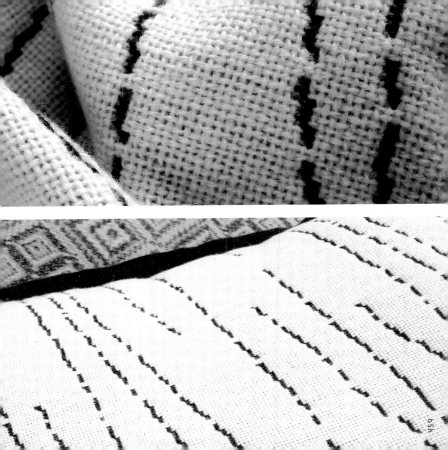

459

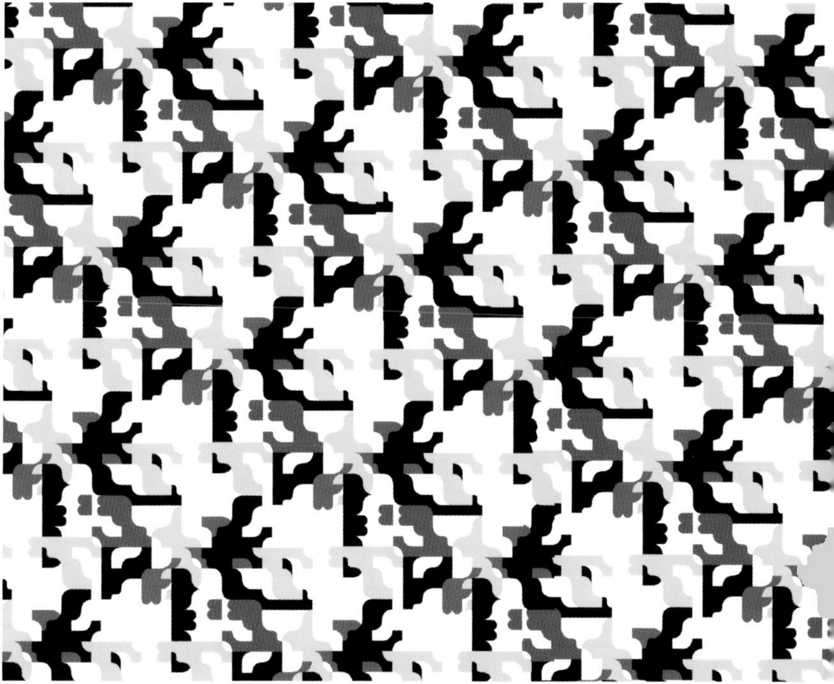

Magdalena Nowak (GER) sweetdreams@hellucinations.de

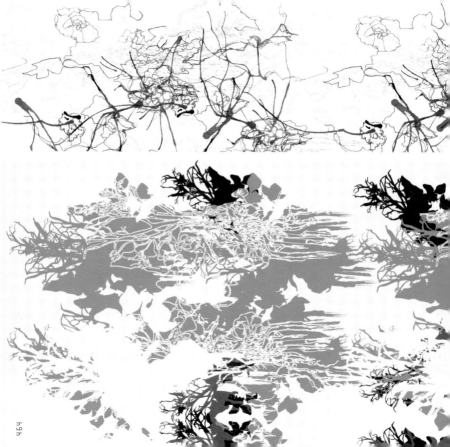

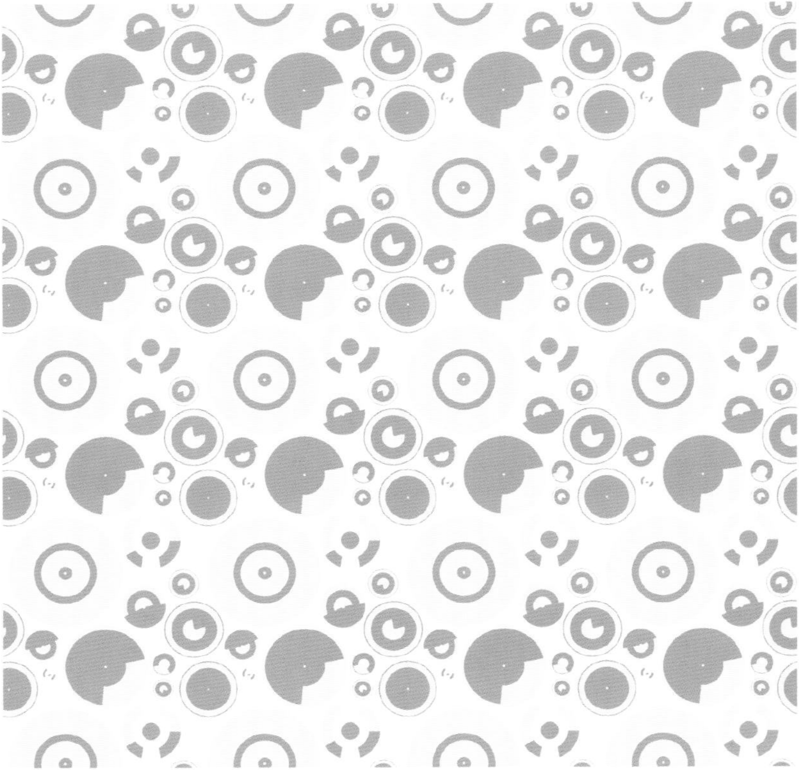

Emil Bertell (GER) www.fenotype.com

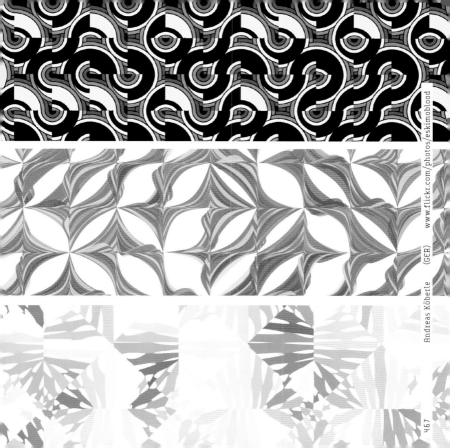

Il-Jin ATEM Choi   (GER)   www.atemmeta.de

469

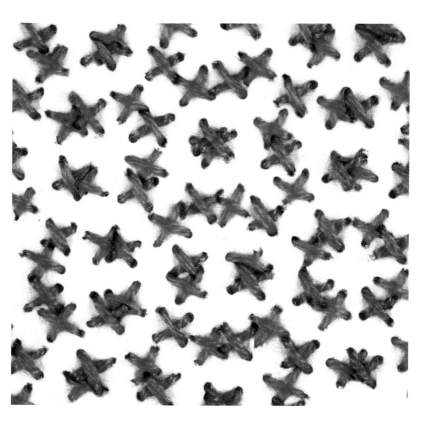

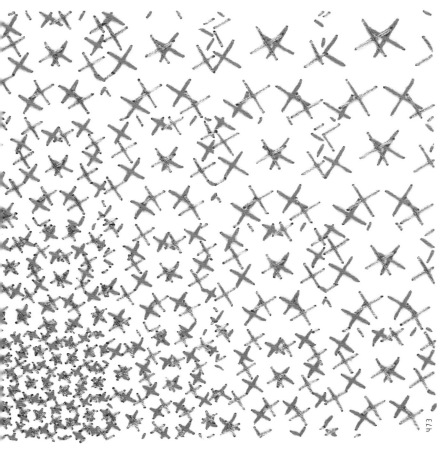

Raquel Quevedo   (ESP)

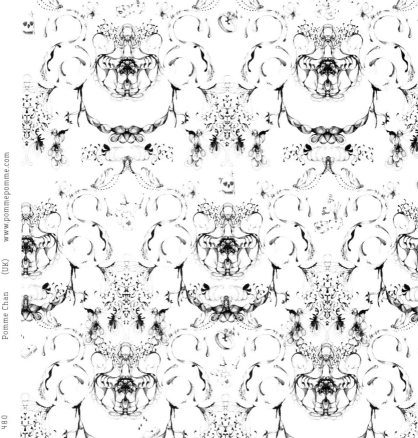

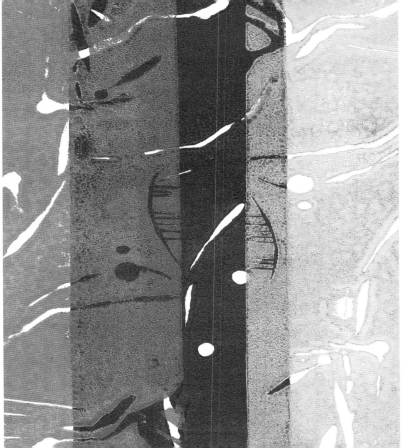

Sabine Reinhart (GER) www.mynetty.de

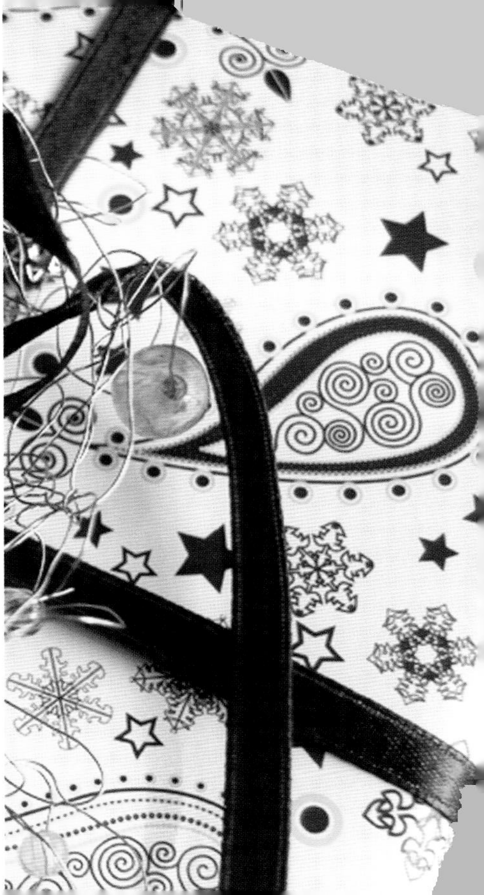

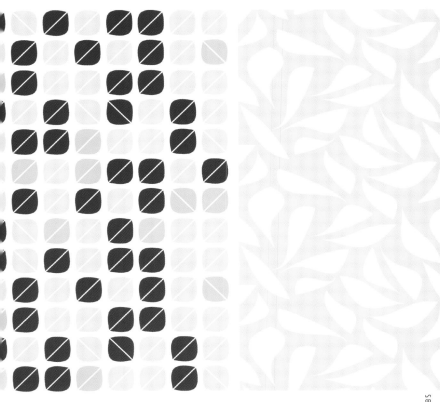

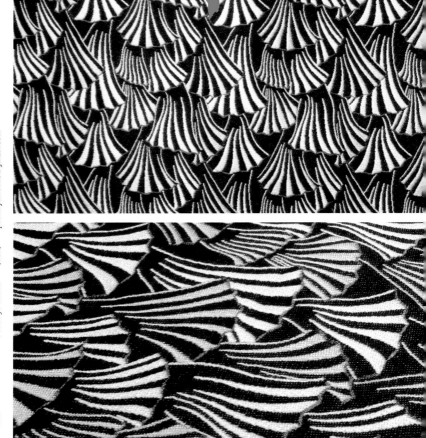

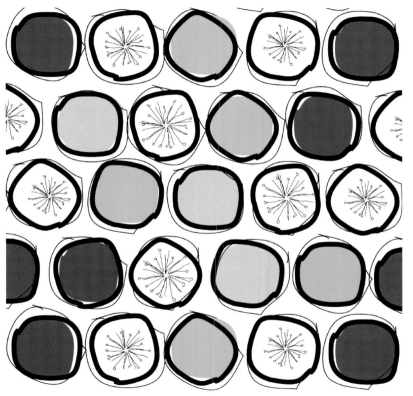

www.absolutezerodegrees.com

Keith Stephenson (UK)

490

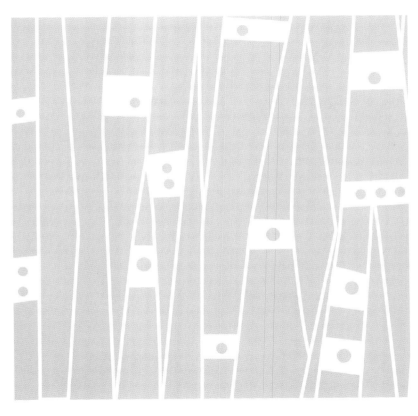

Lisa Engelhardt   (AUS)

Beatriz Lamanna   (BRA)

494

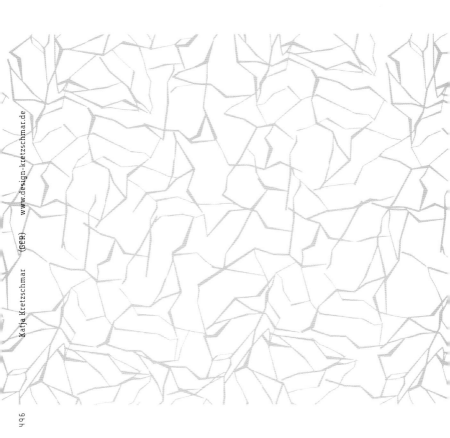

Andrea Forgacs   (GER)   andrea.forgacs@gmx.net

Christoph Ruprecht   (GER)

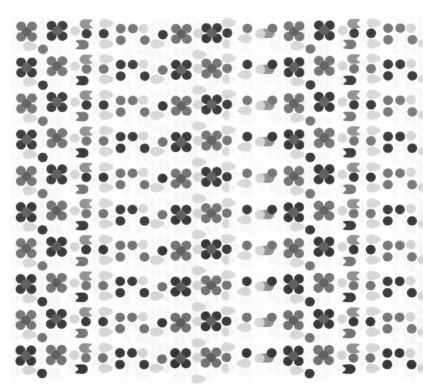

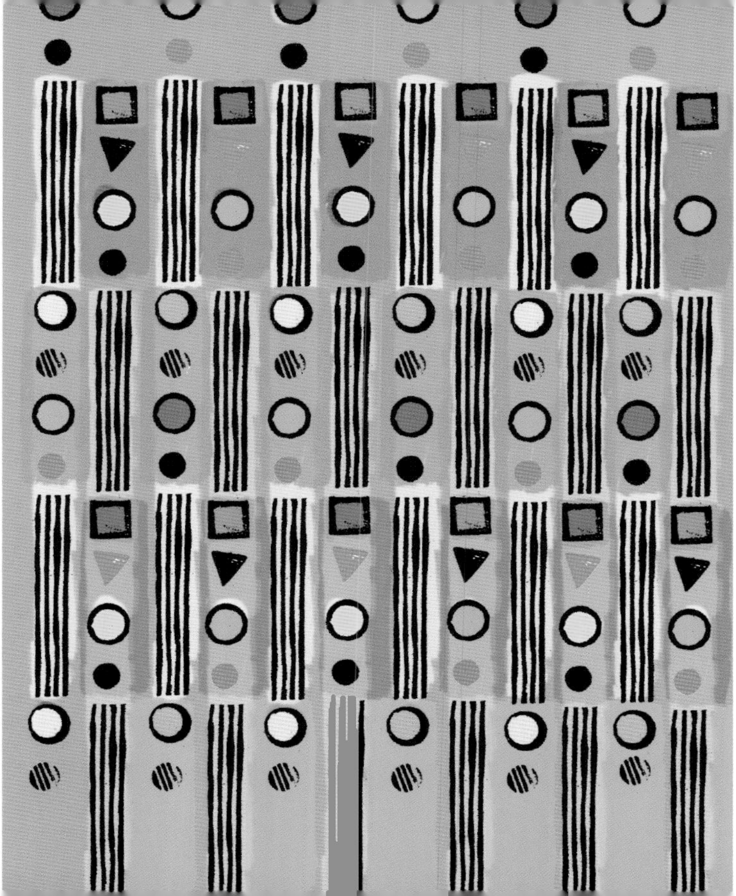

501 Sarah Nussbaumer (USA) www.s-nussbaumer.com

Magdalena Nowak   (GER)   sweetdreams@hellucinations.de

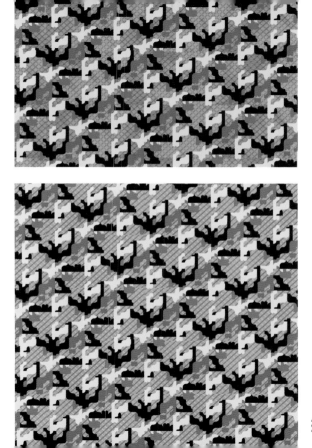

Karl Grandin   (SWE)   www.woo.se/portfolios/var xxxx

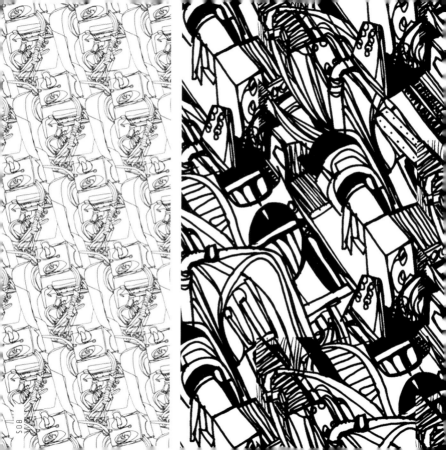

Anna-Maria Niestroj   (GER)   www.anna-maria-niestroj.de

Linus von Moos   (SUI)   www.rips1.ch

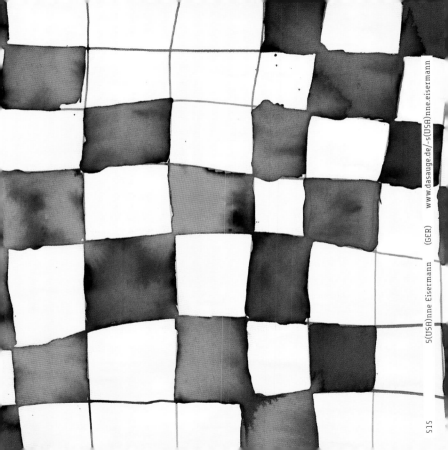

s(USA)nne Eisermann   (GER)   www.dasauge.de/-s(USA)nne.eisermann

Angelica Margain Miranda   (MEX)   margain.a@gmail.com

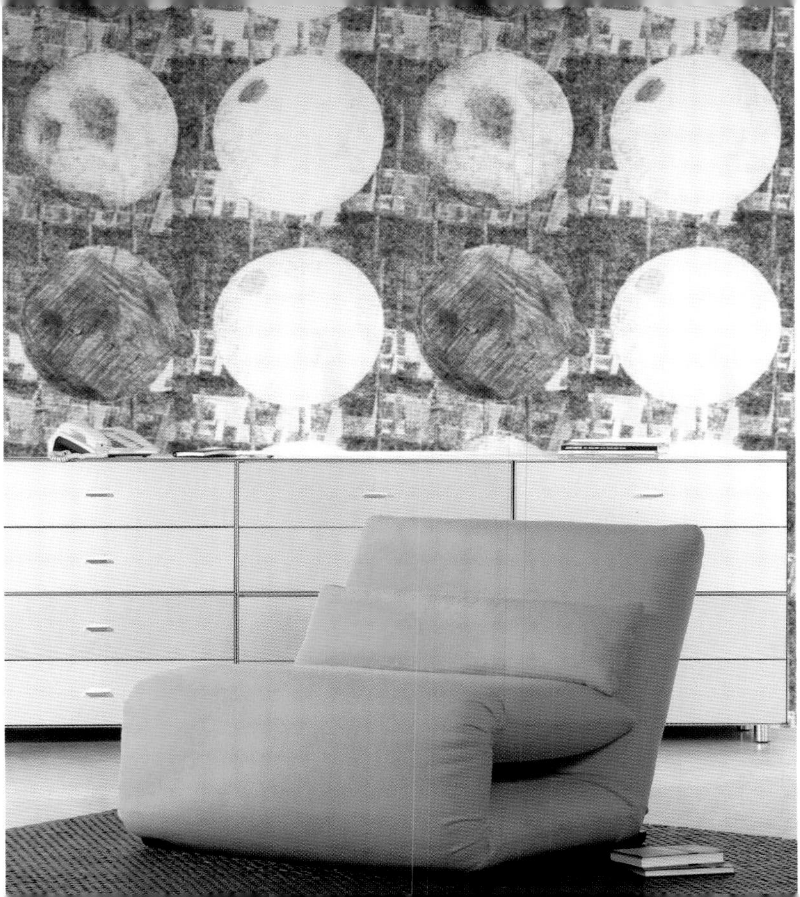

Lenka Petzold (GER) www.lenkapetzld.de

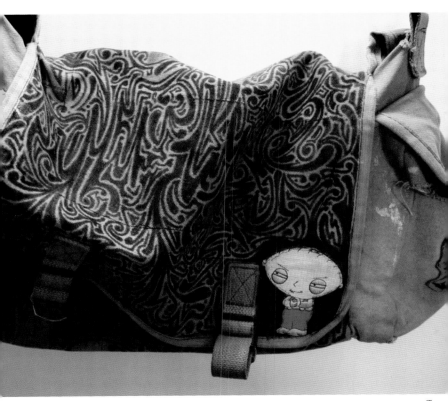

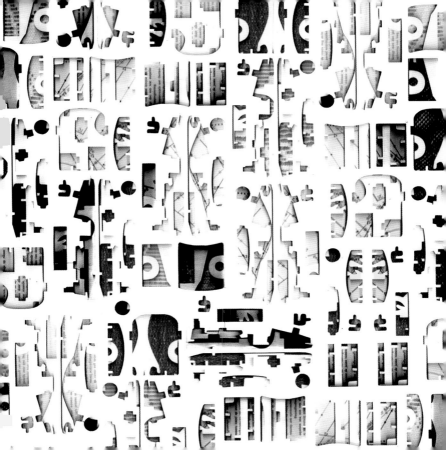

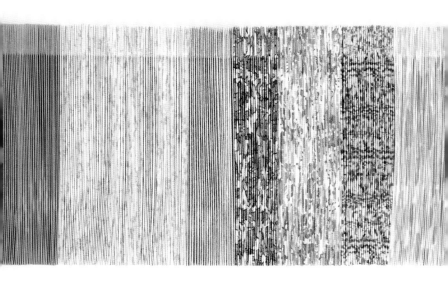

floral

flowers, trees, tendrils

Deirdre Kelaher   (AUS)

528

529

Abhilasha Krishnamurthy (IND) abhilashak@gmail.com

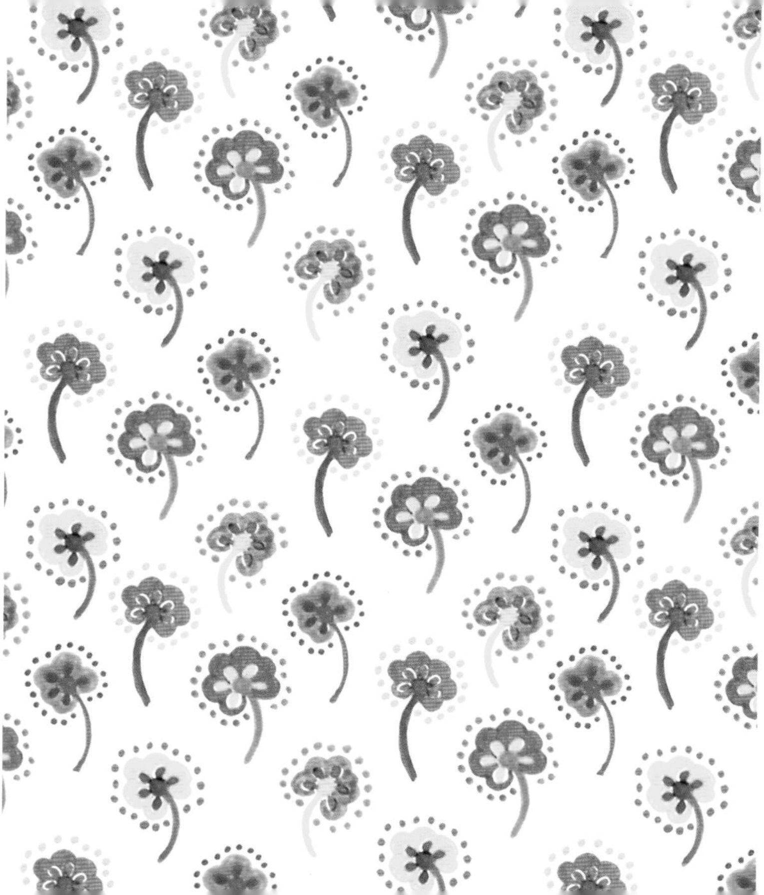

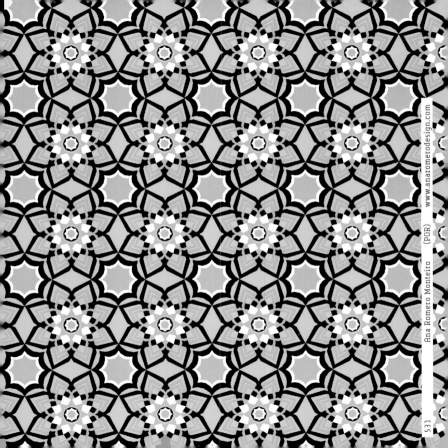

Abigail Borg   (UK)   www.abigailborg.co.uk

Daniel Moraes   (BRA)

S37

Carolyn Gavin   (CAN)   www.ecojot.com

548

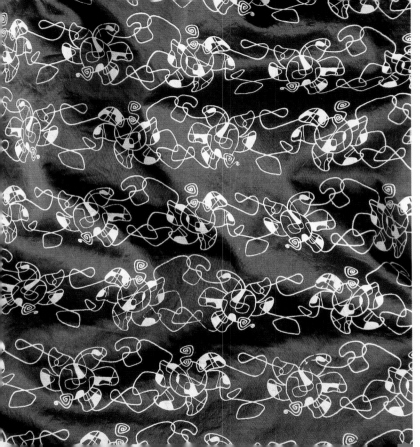

Daniel Moraes   (BRA)

Vartan Tekneyan & Lilo Paleit   (GER)

558

Pomme Chan (UK)   www.pommepomme.com

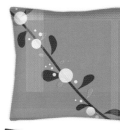

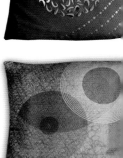

Julia Rothman (USA) www.juliarothman.com

563

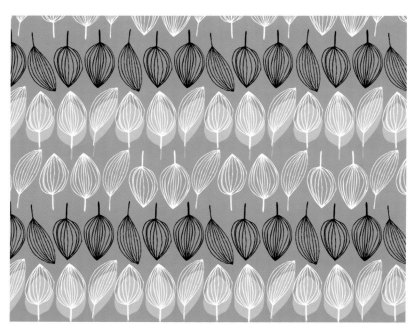

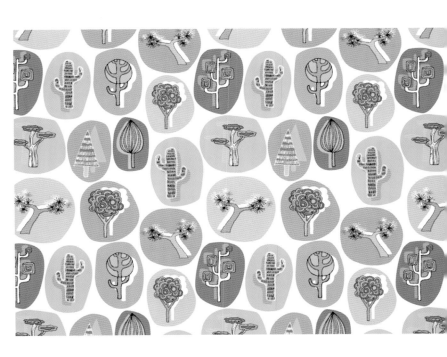

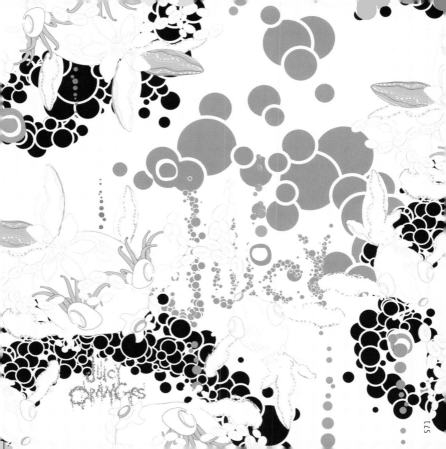

www.sgreendesigns.com

Sarah Green　(USA)

575

Laura Hoyer   (USA)

579

Anna Salander   (NOR)

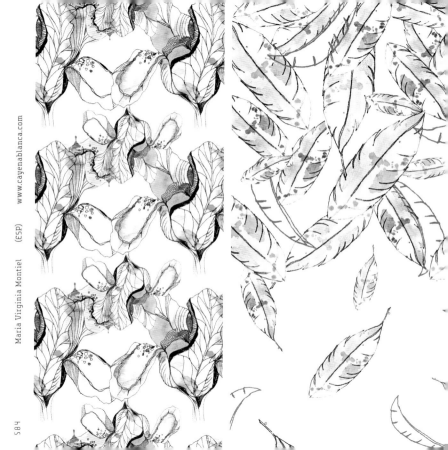

(ESP)

Maria Virginia Montiel

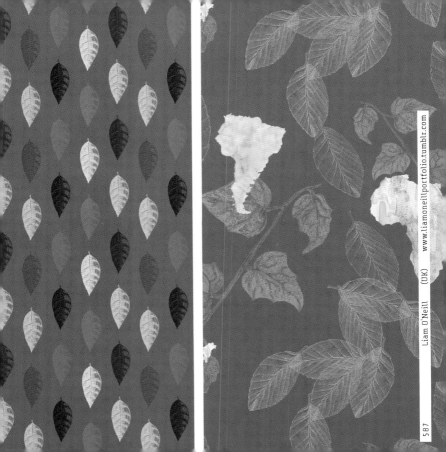

Rachel Holmes (UK) www.behance.net/Rachel_holmes

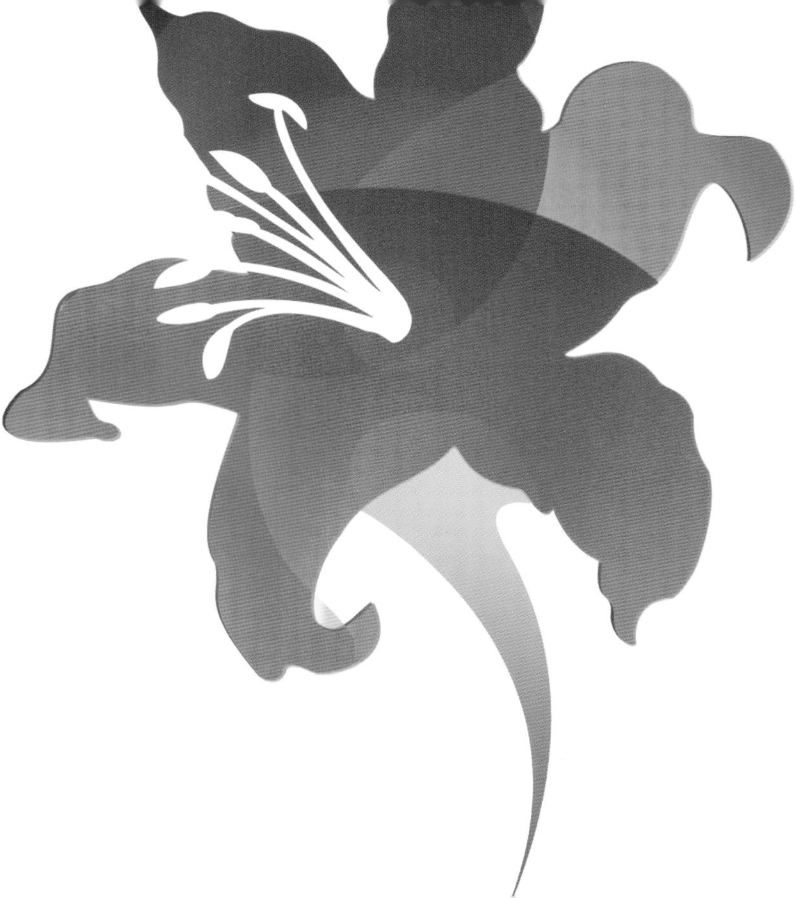

Josephine Kimberling   (USA)

594

Abigail Borg   (UK)   www.abigailborg.co.uk

Sarah Nussbaumer   (USA)   www.s-n-nussbaumer.com

Caroline Wall   (UK)   www.carolinewalldesign.co.uk

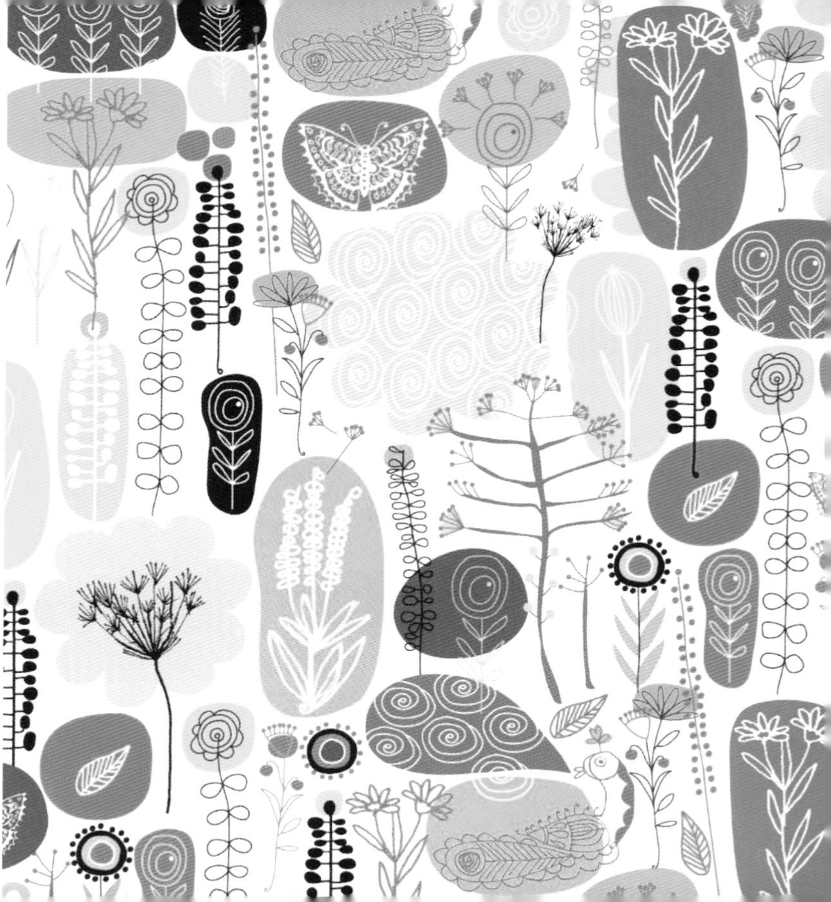

Carolyn Gavin (CAN) www.ecojot.com

"Love is like the sun coming out of the clouds... the best thing about me is you."

"Life is the flower for which love is the honey."
-Victor Hugo

Raquel Quevedo (ESP) www.raquelquevedo.com

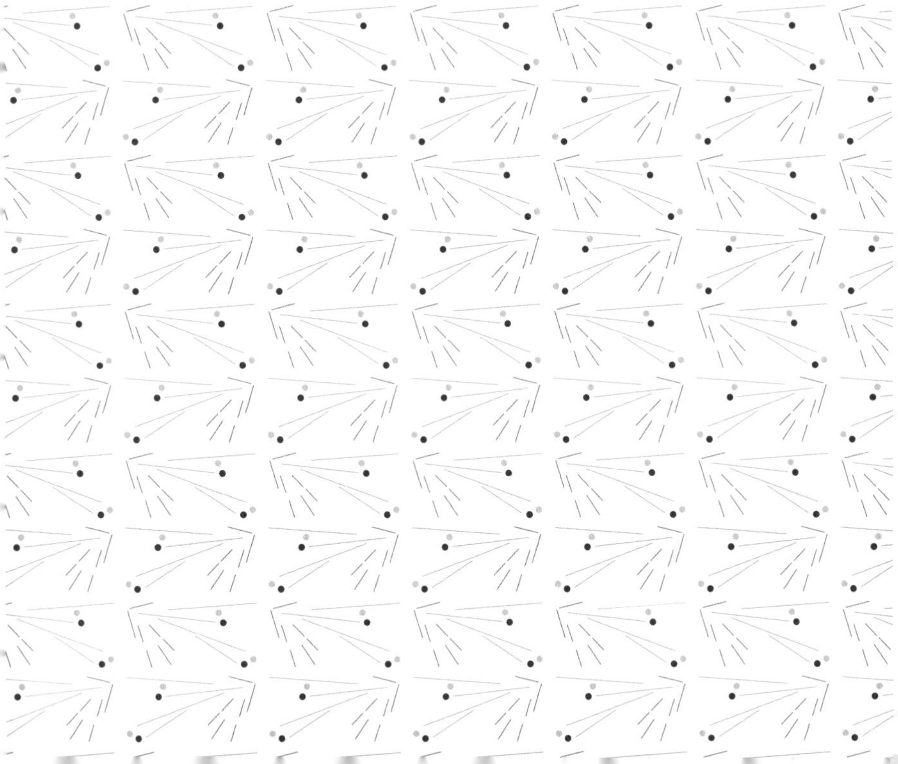

Vartan Tekneyan & Lilo Paleit   (GER)

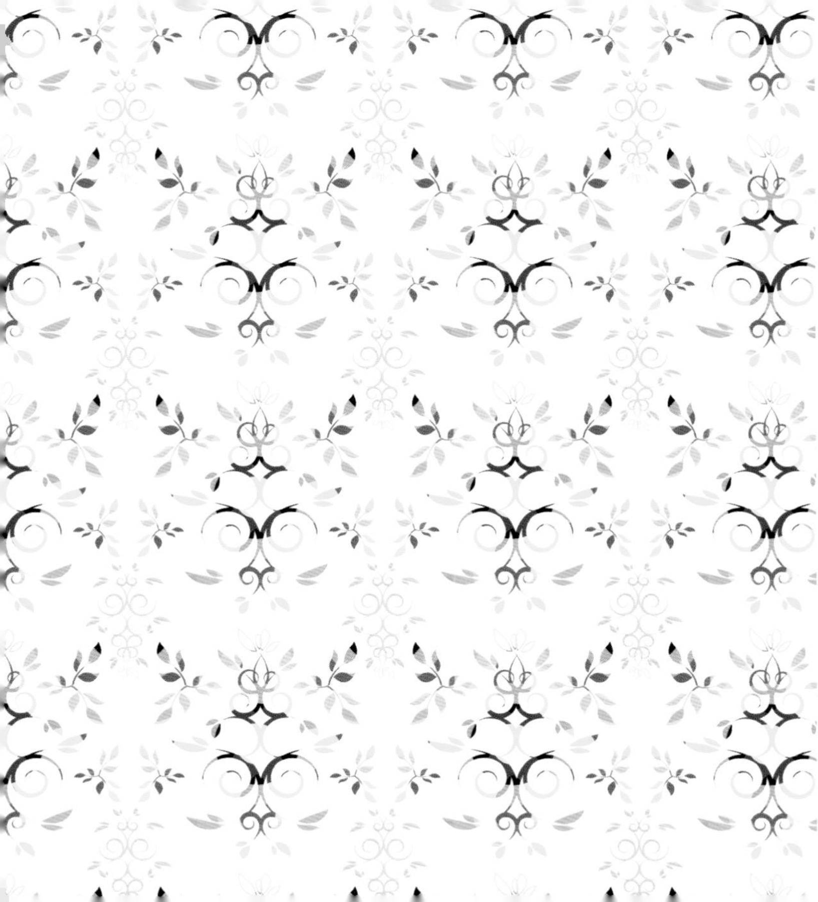

611 Sabine Reinhart (GER) www.patterrific.com

Laura Hoyer   (USA)

626

625

626 Goh Tze Yee (MAS) tyee_10@yahoo.com

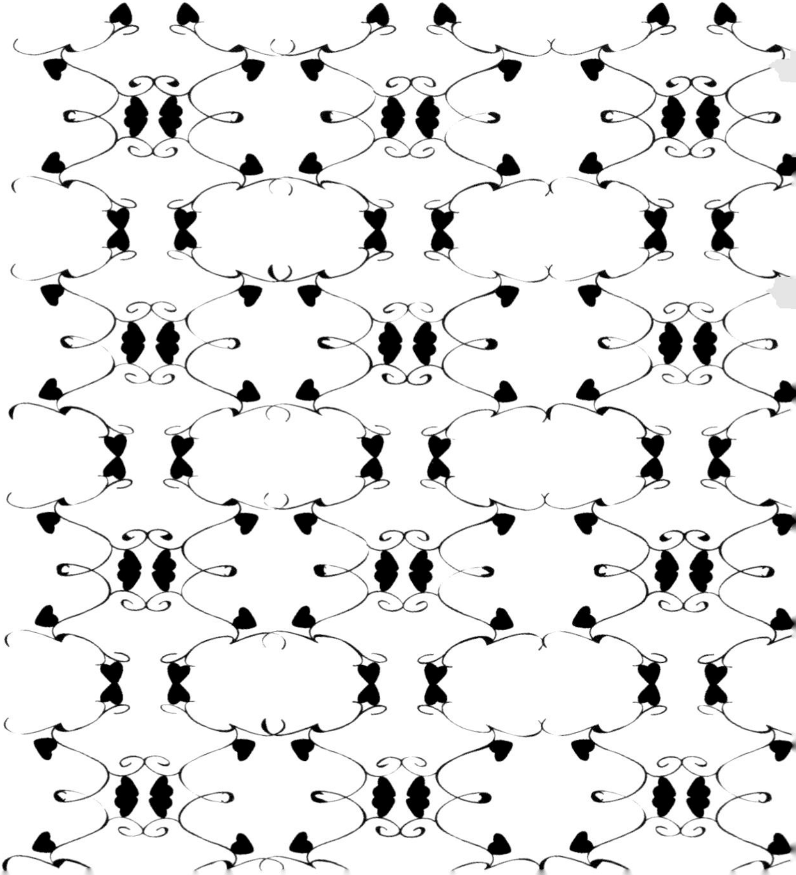

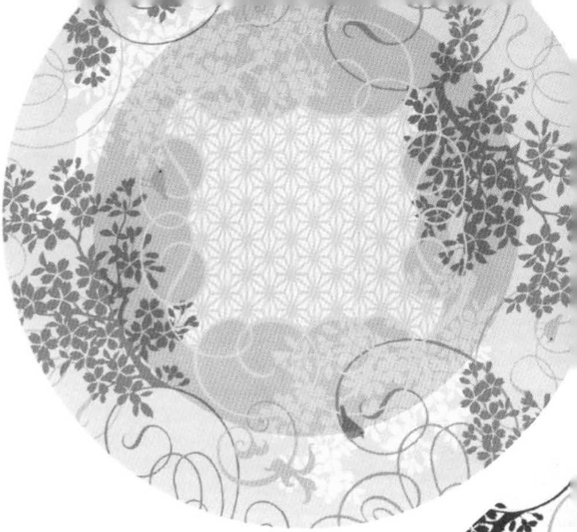

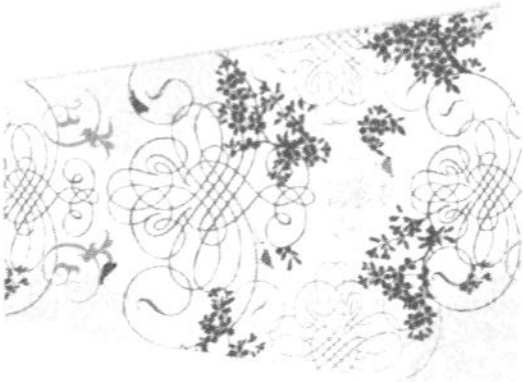

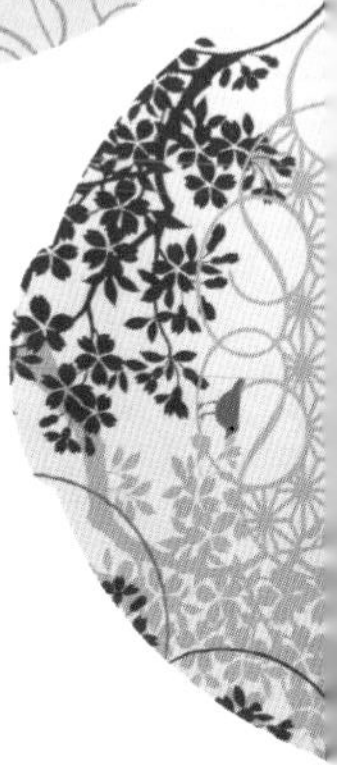

 Macrina B(Usa)To (ESP) macrinab(USA)to-design.com

Beatriz Lamanna   (BRA)   www.nubestudio.net

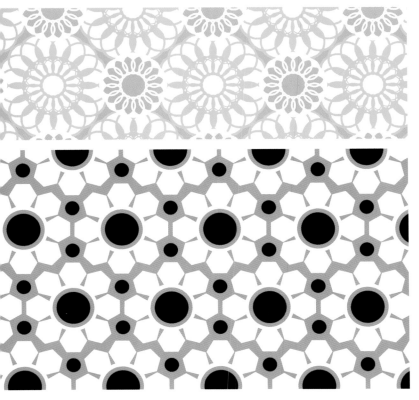

Ana Romero Monteiro   (POR)

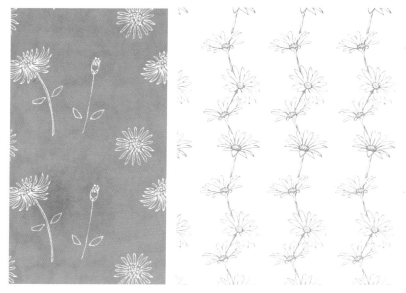

Karen Jinks   (UK)   www.karenjinks.co.uk

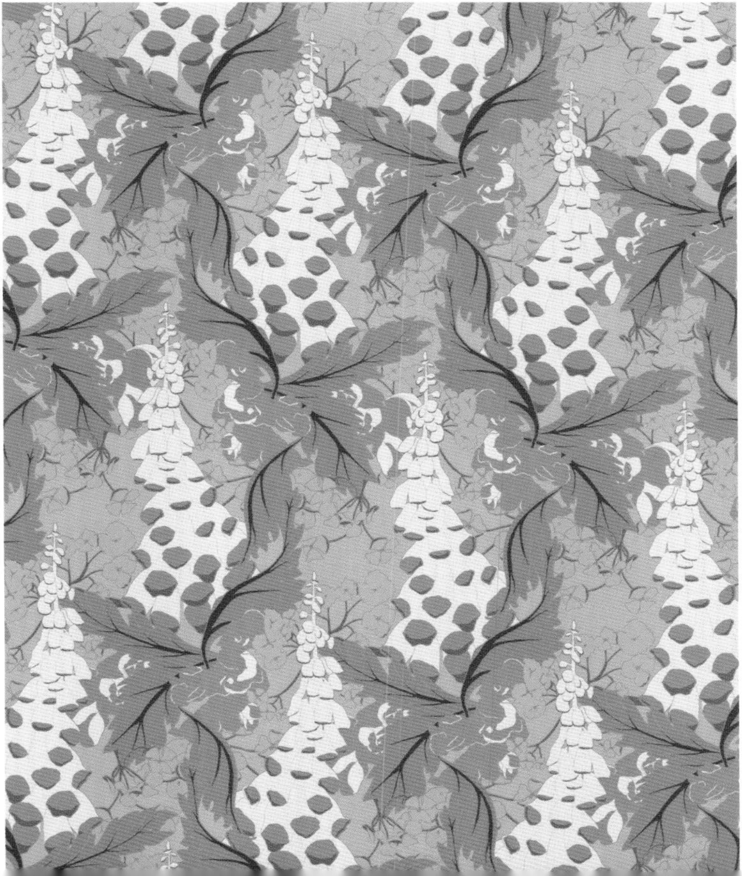

Abigail Borg (UK) www.abigailborg.co.uk

Shannon Lamden (AUS) www.auntycookie.com

Cinzia Cappellazzo   (GER)   www.cinziacappellazzo.com

Annette Taylor-Anderso   (UK)

säenswert
GESCHENKE DER NATUR

Leidenschaft

Blumensaaten Rot
Adonisröschen, Mohn und Elfenspiegel
{GEEIGNET FÜR BALKON & GARTEN}
AUSSAAT VON MÄRZ – MAI

Energie

Blumensaaten Gelb
Schmuckkörbchen, Sonnenblume und Ringelblume
{GEEIGNET FÜR BALKON & GARTEN}
AUSSAAT VON FEBRUAR – MAI

säenswert
GESCHENKE DER NATUR

Gemma Robinson   (UK)   gemmamarierobinson@hotmail.co.uk